MW00620207

AN HONEST WOMAN

A MEMOIR OF
LOVE AND SEX WORK

CHARLOTTE SHANE

SIMON & SCHUSTER

New York London Toronto Sydney New Delhi

100 YEARS
SIMON &
SCHUSTER

1230 Avenue of the Americas
New York, NY 10020

Some names have been changed.

First Simon & Schuster hardcover edition August 2024

SIMON & SCHUSTER and colophon are registered
trademarks of Simon & Schuster, LLC.

Simon & Schuster: Celebrating 100 Years of Publishing in 2024

For information about special discounts for bulk purchases,
please contact Simon & Schuster Special Sales at 1-866-506-1949 or
business@simonandschuster.com.

The Simon & Schuster Speakers Bureau can bring authors to your live event. For
more information or to book an event, contact the Simon & Schuster Speakers
Bureau at 1-866-248-3049 or visit our website at www.simonspeakers.com.

Interior design by Wendy Blum

Manufactured in the United States of America

1   3   5   7   9   10   8   6   4   2

Library of Congress Cataloging-in-Publication Data
has been applied for.

ISBN 978-1-9821-2686-5
ISBN 978-1-9821-2688-9 (ebook)

For P,
who gave me this

"Honest woman. I wish she had been more of a prostitute."
—Alasdair Gray, *1982, Janine*

AN HONEST
WOMAN

I

Roger emailed me in April 2011, when I was twenty-eight years old and he was fifty-four. Our first date was to take place at a Marriott in downtown DC, a city he frequented for his work as a litigator. I arrived at nine in the morning, and when I got there, I realized I didn't have his room number. I called him, but he didn't answer. I'd have to wait.

As I stood in heels and a blue tailored shift on the lobby carpet, while children zoomed around me and Starbucks-guzzling tourists sank into their armchairs, I felt irate and exposed in a familiar way. Work as an escort entails a certain blankness, as can any straightforward physical purpose: shower, pick an outfit, go to a hotel, leave a hotel. I often felt like my body's chauffeur, striding through public spaces with brisk efficiency. In these situations—surrounded by less polished people or forced to loiter in lobbies—I was self-conscious of my conspicuous vehicle. The flattered figure, the tensed calves. A woman alone. Conventional business attire, or what I thought passed as conventional business attire, wasn't intended to disguise my vocation but to imbue it with some legitimacy. I wasn't afraid of being thrown out; I deserved to be there. I was invited. Strangers' opinions didn't matter, but still: I didn't like the way they studied me.

After I checked our email thread and saw that we were

meeting at nine p.m., not a.m., I wrote Roger a note confessing the error, apologizing for the unscheduled phone call, and confirming the evening date. That's all I remember about our first meeting: why and when it didn't happen, and that he was nice about my stupid mistake. I have no recollection of returning that night, though I know I did. I logged the payment and duration in my spreadsheet, and I wrote him an email the next day: "Thank you for a wonderful evening! I cannot wait to see you again." I thanked every client unless they'd done something so wrong that I might decline a repeat.

In Roger's retelling, our second date was when he realized I didn't like wine, so he stopped buying a bottle for our meetings. The third time, he said years later, was when his heart took true notice of me. I was going down on him and he worried I was uncomfortable, so he asked if I wanted to stop or change my position. "Oh no," he said I assured him, lifting my head to speak, "this is very sustainable."

"I have to say that each time I visit with you, I am left wanting to see you more," he wrote after that. I heard this sort of thing all the time, often in more ardent forms. The sentiment came from married men, single men, men who were divorced, men a few years or a few decades older than me, men who were wealthy and men who were rich, men living under secret, crushing debt. Some cried over how much they felt for me, wrote me songs and poems, daydreamed aloud about marrying or impregnating me. I felt highly desired, and I was, verifiably, highly desired.

Coveted, even. There was proof: the messages, the money, the affirmations. I became a sex worker because I suspected, and hoped, it would be this way: a private, minor form of celebrity. An alternate version of myself.

THERE WERE SOME CONVENTIONS in escorting during the early 2010s that are not as common now. Websites featured stock photos of jets and champagne and black Amex cards. The About Me sections listed MAs and PhDs, fluency in at least one foreign language and conversational competence in others. There were women who wrote that they'd grown up in European boarding schools and spent family vacations skiing the Alps, or that they'd given up modeling careers to pursue higher learning and more mentally stimulating work.

It took me years to learn that truth in all advertising is rare. Until then, I worried I wouldn't be able to charge what the other women did, and therefore wouldn't be able to live the lives I imagined they led. It wasn't that I thought I was dull or wholly unappealing, just that I knew my class status. I wasn't cultured or polished, though I aspired to be. I went to a state school for undergrad, and at my more prestigious graduate university, I pursued a master's devoid of utility. My sporadic childhood vacations involved Holiday Inns. I mispronounced words I'd never heard spoken aloud, like "homage," and when I moved from the chicken farming land where I'd grown up to DC, people laughed at my accent. I've still never held a job with a yearly salary or learned how to apply artful makeup. I was too afraid of being caught in a lie to pretend otherwise, so when I composed my site copy, I wrote around my deficiencies and hoped I'd never need to know the protocol for boarding a private plane or be called on to converse in French.

Clients who especially enjoyed the fantasy of the modern-day courtesan—as the most self-serious escorts called themselves— sent courtly, almost formal introductory emails, paragraphs intended to demonstrate their impeccable etiquette as well as brag about their jobs and education. They wanted to make a positive first impression, and also, possibly, mislead us about how forthcoming they were and how much money they intended—or could afford—to spend. They were answering our marketing with their own. It helped that illegality-induced euphemisms tipped the dialogue into affectation: "intrigued" meant horny, "visit" or "spend time with" meant fuck, "friend" meant repeat customer. As in: *I'm intrigued by your website. I would love to visit with you for two hours on Thursday evening in the hope of becoming good friends.*

Some clients took the gallant approach seriously because they wanted to maximize the scenario's dreamy potential. They wanted romance like that of the idealized honeymoon stage of dating. Infatuation and rapture on demand. These were often the same men who enjoyed the ballet and wanted to go to bed at a reasonable hour. They were motivated by sex and expected it, but they also valued having a tastefully dressed, sufficiently bright conversationalist who could pass as a work acquaintance or distant relative if they ran into someone they knew. Once, at the Boston Symphony, I was introduced as the board member of a nonprofit. The lie was bolstered by the fastidiousness of my date, a small, avuncular, elderly man who cooked food for his terrier and played an unglamorous role in local politics.

The majority of clients I met over the years were polite and decent. Roger signed his first message to me "best regards," and he meant it. Why wouldn't he send warm regards to this stranger he hoped to pay for sex? He was a nice guy: a prominent lawyer who'd worked pro bono on a significant environmental case; a proud father who'd twice taken his firm's maximum paternity leave; a husband whose wife kept her last name. He was mild-mannered when not in a courtroom, and based on the stories he told me, he kept a modest, principled air about him there, too, to win over the judge and give dramatic moments more weight. In this way—the professional, calculated deployment of intellect combined with general trustworthiness—we were alike.

ROGER WAS A SERIOUS, outwardly dispassionate man with no penchant for luxury or debauchery. He relied on a single pair of jeans and brandless black sneakers when not dressed for work. His trifold wallet sealed with Velcro. (That couldn't be what he withdrew at client dinners when the check arrived, could it?) He watched corny movies and bad TV and read genre fiction. He attempted chivalry, though his blind spots were many. For years, until a cabdriver admonished him for it, he had me get in first and slide across the back seat so he could get in after. He never once offered to carry a bag, even when we went shopping for something like groceries and left with multiple sacks.

But he was kind, and not snobbish, and unfailingly polite to service staff. He never addressed anyone in anger while I was present, though he sounded stern by default. His voice was gruff and almost artificially low, as if he had trained himself to speak that way. At rest his countenance was unsmiling. He had a full head of hair, an unchanging white beard, heavy cheeks and belly, and he maintained an austere, old-fashioned air of dignity. British novels from the late 1800s usually include a patriarch who reminds me of him.

One of the more incongruous aspects of Roger was that until I met him, and for a short time after, he was a prodigious whoremonger. He traveled constantly for work, and when he did, he'd hire someone, usually someone he hadn't met before and often two someones simultaneously. He'd been with Ashley Dupré before the Eliot Spitzer scandal, just once, in New York, and was struck by her pert declaration of "It's time for you to eat some pussy" while she pushed his head down. He told me there was another girl there, but he didn't mention her name or anything else about her, presumably because she hadn't made a memorable pussy-eating demand.

These assignations went on for a decade or two, yet he'd somehow never had anyone sleep over. Our fourth date was significant because it was his first time spending all night with a woman he'd hired and also my first time traveling for him. We met in New York, and I was unimpressed with our hotel, which I expected to be fancier given that Dominique Strauss-Kahn, an apparently rich and important European, was on trial for assaulting a maid there several months prior.

Roger gave me a massage in the dark—most clients want every bulb blazing, but he turned the lights off before he was shirtless or naked—and while I lay back, he knelt in front of me on the bed, lifted my legs to his face, and kissed them. "I've never kissed the back of a woman's knees before," he said. I'd been tumbling around like a dryer ball in a churn of relentless sexual experience since I started sex work at twenty-one. That he could register something so mundane as a first, let alone that it could *be* a first for him at fifty-four, was bizarre to me. What had he been doing with the girls before me?

I say Roger was incongruous because even when he was hard, even while he was inside me, even when he asked for anal, he wasn't a creature of lust. On the morning after our overnight, he dressed for work and left me unmolested in a hotel robe with room service, though an overnight, in my professional experience, meant sex at least twice. On the occasions when he described a sexual thought of his, it struck me as unconvincing, a non sequitur. (*You* think about sex?) I followed his lead through the standard heterosexual sequence: some kissing, stroking, oral sex for one of us and then the other, culminating in vaginal penetration. He was consistent and dependable in bed and out, with tastes as modest as a monk's. I did not take it upon myself to shake up his routine. He'd seen dozens of prostitutes before we met, and, knee-kissing aside, I doubted that he behaved much differently with me, sexually at least, than he had with numbers six and seven.

While I was on the train to meet him for our first overnight, he emailed to coordinate date number five. Two meetings later, he explained his idea of giving me an ATM card so I could take out my own payments and he wouldn't have to keep cash on hand. It made sense, he said, because "each time I see you, I only want to see you again." He planned for his day-to-day future and liked logistics to be easy; he only booked flights in the morning, for instance, to avoid the cascading delays and cancellations that came in the afternoon and evening. He wanted me to join him on an international business trip, and he told me I could take as much time as I wanted for myself while we were there. "It is one thing to be as selfless and giving as you are for three hours or even an overnight," he wrote. "A trip of this scale is quite different."

I had no idea what he was talking about when he called me selfless and giving. He was an easy client. What was I giving, exactly, and why did he think it was so taxing to give it? He said I was "somewhat of a confessor" to him: "Whatever I say to you, you listen with sympathy and without judgment." But he wasn't divulging terrible secrets. He was just sharing quotidian human experience: frustration and pride at work, tension between siblings. Clients often want to talk as much as or more than they want to fuck, so that part wasn't new to me. The ability to listen was a basic requirement. The piece that didn't make sense was how the other women he'd hired had been so bad at their jobs.

After a year together, he told me he didn't want to hire anyone new anymore. A lot of clients, lying, said the same. Men seemed addicted to pledging monogamy and then violating their unsolicited promise. I think the lie made them feel important, or they thought it was necessary to access something otherwise denied—condom-less sex, lower rates. But I believed Roger. From the start of our relationship, I didn't doubt that he told me the truth. He was reflective enough to understand his motivations, and he shared them with me because his own gratification impelled him to. (For the international date, he encouraged my intervals of solitude and freedom "so that the time we are together is the best possible.") Since he found fulfillment in psychic and emotional unburdening, deceiving me was not in his self-interest. It would have been closing a door he needed open.

Roger was also profoundly concerned with making sure I liked him. He lived in fear of upsetting me and afforded me supernatural powers of omniscience and appraisal. "The fact that you have some regard for me gives me the greatest pleasure," he wrote. "Because I worship you, the smallest crumb you toss in my direction is a feast for my ego."

MEN HAVE AN EASIER time respecting prostitutes than women who hate prostitutes care to admit. There's a line in a Lorrie Moore story: "Her father is of that Victorian sensibility that deep down respects prostitutes more than it does women in general." Men can think more highly of the former than the latter because unlike a civilian woman, a prostitute is direct and therefore honorable, ballsy—forthright, like a man. That's how they see it, anyway. She's forgone weaponized emotions and commitment-focused schemes in favor of an explicit exchange. By acknowledging sex as transactional, she divorces it from perpetual obligation. Isn't there a cliché about husbands who cheat with unpaid mistresses to disastrous effect before they wise up and turn to pros? If not, there should be. The mistress is a lover who must be wooed and tended to. Her demands are mood-influenced, unpredictable, insatiable. She wants the man to forfeit too much for her: his home, his marriage, his good name. She can easily become his enemy and undoer. But the prostitute is not a burden. She only wants cash. She says so up front, then leaves. In her apathetic constancy, the whore is man's "accomplice," says writer Virginie Despentes, who worked as one.

Prostitutes are more public than civilian women, too: public like men because we negotiate with men and because we've refused to play what men see as other women's games, using sex to engineer family and parasitic security. Despentes says that when men dream of being women, they imagine themselves as whores, not as housewives, because they can't fathom giving up their freedom. The whore can roam the streets, stay out at night, sleep late, sleep around, while the wife is burping the baby and washing dishes. Many of my clients liked to imagine being in the position they imagined I was in. I know because they said so, amid their rote leading questions: Didn't I love doing this? Wasn't this an inconceivable delight? This would be their dream job, they said, if they were women. But because they were men, it was not.

My work friends and I mocked them for their self-flattering delusions, their pathetic attachment to the idea that any sex was good sex, that there was never a wrong time or mood for it, and that having orgasms was the whole of the job. These guys acted like we were nymphos incapable of disappointment or disgust—like men, or how men are supposed to be when it comes to sex and perhaps how these men believed they would be if afforded the right conditions. But I think men are attracted to the job for another reason, the same reason I was: being affirmed as an object of desire.

IN 2011, I MET fifty-three new clients, including Roger, and I had 167 dates, twelve of which were with him. We couldn't see each other in the month of December due to his travel schedule and family commitments, but in November, for an early Christmas, I bought him a figurine of the character Bender from *Futurama*, a show we both liked. I'd watched it on repeat one summer with my grad school housemate in our dark, air-conditioning-free rowhome and knew many lines by heart. There was one I thought of with my neediest clients, the ones who wanted to mainline me, pore over me, wring me out into a glass and then drink me: *This—* what we do here, what we have now, who we are to each other in this moment—*is the maximum level of being with me*. Bender, a robot, says it when some tiny humanoid beings who live on his metal body have mistaken him for God and believe that if they die to prove their faith, they'll fully merge with him. They don't understand that the unsatisfying lot they have is as good as it gets and that the allegiance, the love and devotion, is its own reward.

The gift impressed Roger deeply, as I intended it to, and he sent me a picture of the toy posed on the desk in his office. We would have nine more years together, though of course neither of us knew that then, not the depth of his wanting to be with me nor how long it would endure. And over those nine years, I never found him a better present. "I hope you have a wonderful holiday," he emailed, "and that people make you as happy as you have made me."

Though he was not prone to jealousy, he occasionally made reference to his invisible cohort, which meant he thought about them not infrequently. "If the other men you see don't appreciate you as much as I do," he said, "they're a bunch of rotten fools."

II

When I was sixteen, I fell in love with boys, really fell in love with them—the fact of them, the phenomenon— after I took up with a pack of kids who went to my town's other high school. We met because I was in the community theater's annual musical with several of the group's most prominent figures. A few years before, one of my friend's fathers, a director, needed pickpockets for *Oliver!*, and the guys he tapped from his daughter's social circle liked it enough to stick around.

These boys were the right crew to play delinquents. Perhaps because our county was one of the poorest in the state, ranked second in violent crimes and third in homicides, they were not stereotypical theater kids. They were chain-smokers and heavy drinkers before they could drive, though they drove before they could legally drive, too, raised by adults who'd done the same. They skipped school, snuck out, dented already damaged cars, jumped from roofs and moving vehicles, sang loudly, and shouted often. They talked about circle jerks, getting each other off, and comparing size. They knew filthy phrases I'd never heard before and opened weird porn on their computers with a carnival barker's flair. They were regularly, abruptly naked for the sheer provocation of their own bare bodies; they wanted to make girls laugh as they tore through parties, penises flopping like the tongues of panting dogs, before they cannonballed into pools or jumped onto trampolines. And we did—we laughed, and we loved them. Their nakedness never got old, though I pretended it did. I was addicted to their energy, their fearlessness, their intolerance for boredom. They lived more deeply than anyone I'd ever met.

Of course I'd been around men and boys before: my dad, my brother, classmates, teachers, doctors. I'd also read about boys in books, and I'd spent time imagining what closeness with boys would be like. The anticipation wasn't only sexual, though sex was a prominent part of it. In YA novels, my fictional proxies were forever fielding overtures from fellow nerds, more popular peers, stepbrothers or stepdads, even strangers. I expected the same would happen to me once I sprouted boobs and started junior high, but if anyone tried to coerce or proposition me during that time, I was oblivious.

Though I'm not quite an adventurous person, I crave certain types of excitement: strong emotion; intense relationships; the acquisition of secrets; edification, insight, and the opportunity to obtain it through close observation of others. When I started puberty, these budding proclivities expressed themselves to me as horniness, curiosity, and a formless longing. *I just have this big overpowering wanting in me*, I wrote in my journal, *some sort of desire for something I feel like I'm never going to find*. I couldn't understand what I wanted when so much was outside my realm of experience, but I was restless from the call. I suspected boys would be the gateway to that stimulation because they had permission in a way girls didn't, and therefore access to a bigger, freer world. Boys were synonymous with possibility. Possibility was the route to fulfillment.

My male friends proved that hunch right. They were everything I thought they'd be and more. Nothing prepared me for the contagious ecstasy of their pubescent masculinity—not previous experience nor avid reading nor extravagant daydreams. They were perfect human beings to me, godlike because they were limitless, meaning they acknowledged no boundaries or rules. And they were cute, unbearably cute, even—especially—when they were wasted, when they slurred and doled out emphatic affection, put their arms around my shoulders and leaned in heavily, murmured unintelligible words against my ear as they staggered toward another blackout. When the night wound down and we clumped together like littermates on floors or beds, I hoped the next day would never come.

My family didn't do much touching, so the boys' relentless physicality enraptured me. Drunk or sober, they sat in my lap, pulled me onto theirs, touched my hair, leaned against me, lay down over me, picked me up like a bride. They did this with other girls, too; it was personal but not exceptional. "Don't you know how to hug?" one of them, Sean, an incredible hugger, finally asked me in exasperation one day, as if my bad hugs had driven him to the brink. He taught me to hold the embrace and to close the entire space between our bodies, to stop tenting my hips away like I was disgusted by contact. Sean was a dope, but he had a surprising amount of physical intelligence. His signature move, called "The Crow," after his favorite film, was a passionate, tongued kiss to the neck, a rush of rich sensation that tickled and aroused and captivated all at once. My best friend Ali and I discovered this talent and lay beside him, requesting it again and again, laughing in delight as we took turns receiving. Then we ineffectually tried to replicate it on him and each other.

Justin, Sean's best friend, pretended to crack an egg over my head at a party, and I repeatedly requested that afterward, too, mesmerized by the shivery, uncanny motion of his fingers passing from my hair down my back. One night Noah, my crush, sat with me on a porch swing for an hour, cupping my foot and rubbing its arch with his thumb as we talked. I thought I could die happy after that moment: his soft gaze on my face, his hand's warmth on my sole. Incidental contact alone thrilled me. When the boys' bodies met mine with spontaneous intention, it was bliss.

This was a life I'd hardly dared to dream of, one suffused with tribalism, freedom, and exultant chaos. I was like a burr snagged in the fur of a running wolf, swept away at an exhilarating gallop. I would have done anything to be near the boys because when I was, anything could happen—bad things, good things, things I'd never seen or done or thought of before. I loved when things happened. I didn't feel capable of making things happen on my own, but I hoped to be present when they did.

MY BIZARRE SENSE OF who does and doesn't have an ability to "make things happen" carried through into adulthood, when arranging the sort of sex-centered, alone-with-a-man encounters that women are warned against didn't register to me as action. Women sometimes say "I could never do that" about escorting or creating porn—they've said it to me, conspiratorially, in an attempt to express approbation while keeping their distance— but my willingness, or, really, my eagerness, didn't strike me as the driving element. The question wasn't whether I would do it (clearly I would, and did) but if I'd be *allowed* to, given the opportunity, perhaps even solicited. I could fling myself into a situation like a skydiver jumping from a plane, but in my mind, I couldn't foment the situation on my own.

My objective as a teenager was to find the boys, to link up with them because they were the party, they were the event. Years passed, and the objective stayed the same, with the focus shifted to sanction my own creativity: find boys to make a band, find boys to make a movie—find boys because they'd supply the verbs that would propel my life. It wasn't just that they were necessary for sex or romance, though they were for me. More than that, they were the only means of getting at all that life has to offer. They were both the gate and the guides who ushered you through it.

I internalized this notion in total ignorance, like accidentally swallowing a piece of broken glass. And as every shard of glass has an origin, my idea was explicable, born of radical, prescribed passivity. A woman's life is fundamentally inert no matter how busy or accomplished a woman might be because that's the nature of an object, even important or well-traveled objects like the Hope Diamond or the Olympic torch. I had no doubts about the existence of my internal self or the profundity of my soul; I knew I was an individual, a subject, not inherently lesser than. I was blessed with plenty of assertive, admirable female role models throughout my girlhood, and with much affirmation and encouragement. I believed that girls could "be anything" in terms of career, which somehow always meant a doctor, lawyer, or politician. Yet there was no denying women's socially diminished personhood, even among doctors and lawyers and politicians. My agency would only take me so far because women's value had a ceiling.

It seemed women's value also had a source: sex appeal. And the acute, perpetual heartbreak of my young life was that I was not hot when judged against the platonic ideal of hotness: Britney Spears, the most superlatively sexy teenager who ever had or ever would exist. By the time I was sixteen, she dominated pop culture so completely that it was impossible to recall any era before her bare midriff and knowing eye contact. Britney was everything I wasn't and never could be: petite, blond, taut, an incredible dancer. I understood why she was a perfect sex object, but I was still surprised that Sean kept a poster of her on his bedroom wall and claimed he dreamed of taking her alleged virginity. For him, or anyone, to buy into the fantasy left me crestfallen even as I intuited that its crudeness was central to its appeal. When I first saw the video for "I'm a Slave 4 U," in which she gropes her torso, grinds against her partner in low-cut jeans, and pants and heaves from under a pile of people as sweaty and bronzed as she, a blend of exhaustion and torment washed over me. Britney kept raising the bar for how provocative a person who was not a girl, not yet a woman could be. She represented a degree of aesthetic perfection and sexual prowess that seemed compulsory yet permanently out of my reach.

But I had to try to approximate it. I regarded beauty as absolute, a quality as objective as a quantity, but I also knew a person's appearance was changeable, which meant beauty might be attainable for me despite an unbeautiful start. Teen movie makeover montages were one reason for my optimism. Pure hope and naivety were others. (Like millions of generic-looking young women, I entertained the possibility that I would be scouted by a modeling agency at the mall someday, and it would turn out that I'd been gorgeous all along—the hicks of my hometown just couldn't see it.) A Clinique employee at a local department store also played a memorable role when I asked for her help re-creating an exotic eye look I'd torn from a magazine. It was a post-holidays winter weeknight, and the store was empty, so she had time and was bored enough to chat with me about the transformative powers of artifice as filtered through an anecdote about a high school classmate of hers who appeared in *Playboy* after graduation. "It's incredible what they can do with lighting and airbrushing," she said, shaking her head in exaggerated disbelief, "because that girl did *not* look like that in real life."

"Really?" I asked, desperate for her to say more.

"God no," she replied. "She was one of the homeliest girls in our class."

At fifteen, I convinced my father to pay for braces to close the gap in my teeth. (My mother, his ex-wife and my primary caregiver, would never have endorsed such a vain and expensive frivolity.) It was the era of heroin chic, so I became anorexic to the point of amenorrhea and, despite my hatred of sports, joined intramural teams every semester to cover for my obsessive exercising. I counted calories and tried caffeine pills, diuretics, and ephedra. It took every tactic to keep my body from expanding like rising dough, to continually punch it down. A doll-faced girl I worked with at the movie theater helped me stick with purging. "Do you ever worry about being fat?" she asked me once, distress in her searching blue eyes. She'd been hospitalized before and seemed to miss the validation of those days. "Like truly fat? It's my biggest fear."

My father reinforced the primacy of visual appeal, or perhaps instilled it with his frequent commentary on women's bodies. His appraisals were ubiquitous and usually complimentary, a fixture of my life from my earliest memories. Many times as a child I sat in the front seat next to him while we drove by a woman jogging or walking or gardening, and he announced his approval in an voice intentionally frilled with silliness: "She's keeping herself fit," or "I see this young lady is out enjoying the weather." "Fine filly" was common praise. The assessment was delivered in a specific tone of commendation, like he was the benevolent, democratically elected Mayor of Women, verifying that they'd fulfilled their aesthetic duty and taking pride in his civic-minded populace. He told me he'd chosen my first name because it belonged to a strikingly beautiful blond woman he saw once at the pool when he was a teen.

I suppose I rewarded him for his behavior, though I don't think I comprehended the true content of these lines. They seemed to me to be non sequiturs, absurdist quips made to pass the time. When I first registered his calling a woman "a tart," I laughed and laughed, and like any comedian, he was delighted. Yet despite his tongue-in-cheek delivery, repetition indicated that the sentiment was sincere. I saw that he stayed on alert, looking out for a woman who was worth looking at. He didn't intend to do harm with his habitual judgment. He didn't recognize that his attitude was capable of inflicting harm. Yet he felt entitled to do as he did, and entitlement is aggression compressed like a barbed spring beneath an expectation. He taught me that women could never escape male notice and evaluation, not even married mothers on a Sunday morning, weeding their front yards.

WHILE HE CAN BE faulted for his methods or the age at which my lesson began, my father's instruction was sound. I was a curly-haired ten-year-old when curly-haired twelve-year-old Chelsea Clinton became the first daughter and was publicly savaged for her looks. Famously, Rush Limbaugh called her a dog. Five years later, during the Monica Lewinsky scandal, I took driving lessons with a man who listened to Rush in my car. We were on a curvy road with a speed limit (forty miles per hour) that intimidated me when the radio host launched into a pornographic rant about cigars and the twenty-four-year-old brunette drowning in nationwide scorn for her sexuality and her dress size. I remember this because I wondered if the instructor would be embarrassed enough to change the station. (He wasn't, apparently, embarrassed at all.) There was no question that failing to be beautiful was the most egregious crime a woman could commit, and having sex while doing it was the second.

Meanwhile, every piece of media I consumed indicated that a boy having sex with you, or pressuring you for sex while you demurred, was the defining moment of initiation into womanhood, an eruption that rent the fabric of ordinary life—the sort of big bang from which entire histories were formed. Every opportunity for sex was a potential fork in the road of a girl's life. That made "going out" with a guy the ultimate adventure, one of the only proper adventures available to girls as far as I could tell.

Bodily anxiety occupied such a prominent place in my consciousness that it colored how I understood (or misunderstood) everything. My insecurity, in concert with the requisite teenage sensitivity to hierarchy, formed a feedback loop of confirmation about my deficiencies. Even my friendship with the boys—the shape of it, the quality—I saw as predicated on an absence of lust, which then made the joy of fraternity painful and confusing. "Man, Heather is, like, perfect," the alpha, Justin, said once of another girl whose platonic company he enjoyed. He cast a glance around his audience in the car, making sliding eye contact with each of us, then shook his head, grinning like he was about to tell a joke. "I'd be in love with her if she weren't such a fucking dog."

WHILE THE GUYS' OTHERNESS seemed primal and unteachable, the girls of the group were apart from me, too. They knew so much that I didn't about style and flirtation, and their friendships predated me. They were impatient, suspicious, and alluring, more imperious and mature than any adult. The boys spoke to the room, but the girls spoke among themselves, and though the boys' humor could be crude and bluntly hurtful, the girls' disdainful evaluations landed like expanding bullets. I thought it was ridiculous that they were so easily offended by the guys' jocularity when they were clearly the meaner ones.

Despite their intimidating nature, the girls and I had good times together. During a slumber party one of them made me laugh so hard I peed my pants, and I had to borrow a pair of the host's pajama bottoms. We wrote elaborate stories for each other about the group, sublimely absurd auto-fan fiction in which everyone, all fifteen or twenty of us, chugged alcohol in Justin's station wagon during road trips and had filthy, loving sex with our crushes. We emailed and spoke on the phone and met for one-on-one walks around our neighborhoods. It meant something every time they were kind to me. "You're so cute, Charlotte," one of them told me on Halloween, while I was in a costume so low-effort it was unrecognizable as such. "You don't need to go as anyone else because you can just be your cute self." She wasn't saying it in a cruel way; we were still friends then. I wrote that in my journal, too.

But I allied myself, quite obviously, with the guys, and eventually whatever closeness I'd had with the girls largely evaporated. Male acceptance and my reciprocal allegiance marked me as a traitor, a fact that both gratified and saddened me. In their senior year burn book, the girls coded the circumstances of my betrayal in the most emotionally accurate and insulting way they could, by dedicating two pages to calling me a stoner slut. It didn't matter that I wasn't that into weed or that I had far less sexual experience than they. I smoked to be with the boys, and I was alone with the boys when we smoked. How happy I would have been, or so I thought then, if what they wrote were true.

Shedding one's sex appeal was a prerequisite to bonding with the boys, so any given girl's hotness prevented her from relaxing into affinity as I did. The boys threw themselves into sexual pursuits in ways that friendship doesn't require or profit from. They narrowed, became both duller and sharper versions of themselves, shuttering some aspects of their personalities while hosing gasoline on others. Hot girls were perpetually regarded with an objective instead of enjoyed just as they were. *Jess and I vow to hang out with the guys more often (just us)*, I wrote in my journal one summer. *It is our goal to be genderless friends. I slip into that easily. But she's too attractive to them to fill that role, as much as she would like to. I am not sure if I should be envious or pleased.* Distance was the cost, or the penalty, for desirability.

I could be close to the boys, but within limits—a lush field enclosed by a fence, held near while kept in check. The boys either tolerated or cared for me—some of them even loved me—but they didn't *want* me, didn't pine for or obsess over me. Sheer luck had brought me to them, and then my personality overcame, or at least compensated for, my plainness. I could fill the role of a neutral but sympathetic ear—a confessor—because their discourse with me wasn't polluted by desire. But I didn't want their opinion of me to be tinged with pity or disdain for my homeliness. I wanted them to think I was gorgeous and sexy because I wanted to *be* those things—even if I also didn't want the presence of those qualities to ruin what we had. Were these treasures mutually exclusive? I wanted total access to a boy, not this system of borders and parceled-out segments, but I wasn't sure that was possible, for any girl.

I heard how adults talked about high school. It was a singular, strange, magical time that couldn't be replicated in adult life, so what would I lose when it ended? Grown women and men weren't supposed to be friends. They were supposed to be lovers and adversaries, linking their lives despite fundamental incompatibility because of sexual need. To be friends with a guy who didn't want to sleep with me was to hack the usual heterosexual imperative, but with diluted results, and I despaired of repeating it after graduation. Maybe lots of guys would like my personality if they got to know me, but why would a man spend time around a woman in the first place if he didn't want to sleep with her?

WHEN I WAS SIXTEEN, my father demanded two pieces of information from me: my status as a virgin and my status as a lesbian. One of the boys, Tyler, was having a "tent city" party on his parents' property, a large stretch of grass behind their house too big to be called a mere yard. I asked my mom if I could go and was told no because the event would be coed and insufficiently supervised. Artlessly, transparently, I then asked if I could spend the night at my best (girl) friend's house instead, and my credulous mother said yes. She recounted this to my father during his evening call, which was a fixture on the nights when my brother and I weren't with him, after he asked why I wasn't at home.

He hunted for me late that Friday night and eventually pulled me from a tent as I, drunk, insisted one of my friends tell him I wasn't there. My father took me back to his house, the house that was not quite my home, and I begged him not to tell my mother where he'd found me. He said he'd consider it—but only if I cooperated with his interrogation. And the first thing he needed to know was if I was a virgin. I told him I was, which was the truth. Proud of his policing, he still ratted me out to my mom.

Years later, in my mid-twenties, I spoke in passing to a youth counselor and sex education expert who expressed dismay at occasions when authority figures try to "force a disclosure" from a young person. I held on to the phrase because it identified why I felt so wronged that night. My father and I didn't have a close relationship, but that didn't stop him from using his authority to demand I keep no part of myself private. Before I could drive, when I was still young enough to be held to the terms of the shared custody agreement, he read anything I brought to his house: my diaries, short stories I composed for myself and my friends. I only found out he did so because I overheard my brother telling my mom. My father believed he deserved to know whatever he cared to know about me, and I felt violated accordingly, especially because he was someone I (correctly) didn't trust. I was exposed in order to be judged and shamed and kept in my place as subordinate.

My virginity was already a source of consternation for me, and my father's next question affirmed that the only reason a sixteen-year-old wouldn't have taken a dick was if something was wrong with her. "Are you gay?" he asked.

My dad was obsessed with appearances—for years, he'd told me that his long-term girlfriend's weight was a factor in his reticence to marry her—so it makes sense that these were his worst anxieties: *Are you a slut? Are you a lesbian? Who wants you? Are you wanted?* He expected that a big part of fatherhood would involve social display—sometimes it seemed to be the only part he liked. But that couldn't be true if I were a freak. I'm sure he wanted me to date an unobjectionable white guy for a few years and for that guy's parents to be friendly with my own. It would have placated him to have just one picture of me and a boy in an awkward embrace at homecoming so he could show it to coworkers as proof that I was normal and therefore he was, too. He wasn't angling for actual involvement in my life, only attempting to collect ceremonial scraps of information he could wave in front of his peers to confirm he was one of them, that he was doing a good job.

That was the first but not the last time I was on the receiving end of an older man's admonishments about my singleness. Similar confrontations were instigated by clients and taxi drivers, teachers and prospective bosses—any stranger or acquaintance who asked if I had a boyfriend and then demanded to know why not. These tedious ordeals never failed to gall me, especially during the times when I really *didn't* have a boyfriend. It was like being asked to explain why no one came to my birthday party. They thought their questions were some type of compliment, but my romantic life was none of their business, and their probing only poured salt in my conviction that I wasn't hot, that I was failing at one of the most crucial things a woman should be.

MY SENSE THAT I wasn't sexually appealing could have kept me from sex work, but instead, I think, it drove me to it. I wanted so badly to be proven wrong. Optimism kept peeking up like the sun, rising in answer to every night of self-doubt. I visited Manhattan a few times in high school, and the remarks I received on the street there felt not like harassment but appreciation. It wasn't quite being offered a modeling contract at the mall, but it was an indication that outside my small town, I could receive a different reception. The attention of the right men might transform me, or rather, reveal me.

At twenty-one I started working on webcam. I was a disaster on-screen: green, graceless, with a body too long and too soft.

When it came to beauty rituals, my ignorance ran deep. My hair had been written off as unmanageable since I was a child, and I was hopeless with makeup. I had no instinct for what flattered my figure or what colors suited me best, and it took an embarrassing amount of experimentation on camera to figure out which postures displayed the important parts of my body without folding my stomach into rolls.

It fell to AJ, my callous manager, to initiate me into conventional femininity. "Get a spray tan, dude," he said, gesturing his un-ashed cigarette in disgust at my pale skin, the baseball hat covering his baldness worn backward as always. "Buy a wig." These tactics had never occurred to me, though my dark curly hair looked weird and dimensionless on-screen under the fluorescent lights. My problems seemed unsolvable to me, despite the insight shared by the woman at the Clinique counter those years before. I wasn't familiar enough with the tools to solve them.

I started making more money after I doused myself with bronze tint every two weeks, applied black drugstore eyeliner with a heavy hand, and found a platinum blond bob like the one Julia Roberts wears at the start of *Pretty Woman*. These tactics were not especially difficult or time-consuming, and I dispensed with tanning, the most expensive element, once I established a coterie of regulars. I played with the lengths and colors of the cheap wigs I wore. My makeup skills never really improved, but it didn't matter much given the quality of the streaming image.

At three a.m., when my shift ended and I pulled off the

synthetic hair, my reflection in the bathroom mirror was tantalizing and off-putting in equal measures. My tits puffed out of my ill-fitting bra and my natural hair mashed against my skull like I were a newly hatched bird, waxy lipstick smeared, the deep-throating-induced dried tear trails on my cheeks half flecked with mascara. This—the absurd polarity, sexy and repellant elements united on the tableau of my body—was the most honest portrait I'd seen of consumable beauty, of patriarchal womanhood. It was so easy to go from one extreme to the other, and neither state seemed more meaningful or real.

Eighteen months later, when I began work at an erotic massage incall, I saw that even without the beautifying accessories, an average body could be desired, or more than desired. Exalted. Craved. Some men on the webcam site droolingly obsessed over aspects of myself that I'd thought were grotesque, like my breasts, and that was an astonishing revelation for someone who'd fretted over each potential flaw as a barrier to being loved, from the gap between her two front teeth to a half-inch spider vein on her calf. But receiving worshipful attention in person from clients who could see every bit of cellulite, touch every stretch mark and scar, was surreal. I was beginning to suss out what an older escort later confirmed: you can look any way and charge any amount and someone, somewhere, will be happy to pay. Men's tastes were so expansive, their range for arousal so broad. Why hadn't anyone told me?

This phenomenon seemed different from (though related

to) the common social depiction of men as perpetually horny demons who want to put their penises in anything that moves and plenty of things that don't. When I got to know male desire well, I could see the sincerity there. It was usually an authentic response that fed but also existed separately from one's level of general horniness, which wasn't the same for each guy anyway. Men's wide-ranging, easily triggered appreciation felt wholesome and joyous, not contemptible or slimy, nor foisted on them by an urgent, uncontrollable will to ejaculate. It wasn't that they would accept or make do with any body, though sometimes that was the case, but that they were capable of celebrating and adoring almost any body—men as a group, I mean, straight men as a mass. They could be compelled by obvious embellishments, like blond hair or implants, as my webcam work taught me. But in most contexts, imitation of the narrowest beauty standards wasn't necessary. Their enthusiasm was too big for that.

I doubt that anyone *could* have told me this precious information in my teen years, though. I was too blinkered by half-truths to hear it. When I dwell on my adolescence for more than a moment, I gradually recall the boys who did ask me out and my concomitant certainty that they did so out of a lack of other options and general wrongheadedness. I knew boys could like my personality, but attraction to a girl was not supposed to be about that, and I shot them down instantly because their interest in me embarrassed us both. I took my dowdiness as a fact and not a theory.

Later in my career, some of the compliments I received could be explained away as clients selecting me based on their preferences; they liked tall women, for instance, and I checked that box. Advertising websites sorted girls by hair color, cup size, build, and self-reported age. But at the incall, a man might show up just because he trusted the agency and I was the only one working that day. Not every client I saw loved me or even liked me, but they rarely showed evidence of reacting to my looks as harshly as I feared they would. They didn't imply that I weighed too much or wasn't pretty enough to pay. Surely as customers they were in a prime position to express this if they felt it. Every time I received an indication that virtually no one else held me to the standards I held myself, it lessened my self-recrimination.

THE BIGGEST MYSTERY AT the incall was Theresa, a popular one-day-a-week girl who was described by her starry-eyed clients as wonderful beyond words. Her appeal was superlative and uncontested, as if she were the LeBron James of jerking guys off, and though they didn't entirely ascribe her allure to her appearance, I assumed she was uncommonly lovely. I never managed to meet her since there was usually just one person on the clock at a time, but my coworker Emily did. She was amazed by the woman behind the myth—her yellow teeth and bland face, her cigarette smell and lank hair. "She is not cute," Emily said.

That Theresa wasn't very attractive, that she might actually be *un*attractive by the usual rubric, was a circle I couldn't then square, but Emily herself cast a similar spell. She wasn't ugly—she was a tan brunette in her early thirties with a belly button piercing on her enviably lithe torso. Yet her immediate effect on men was well out of proportion to her looks. Wherever we went together, whether to a concert or a restaurant or simply standing on the street, someone hit on her. She'd fielded something like eight marriage proposals since high school. Her boyfriend was a handsome, loving, endlessly patient man whom she described as the type of guy you'd want to be with if you had cancer, and she cheated on him with some of her many other options because he wasn't assertive enough in bed. That was why I didn't doubt the veracity of her assessment of Theresa; Emily had nothing to be threatened by.

Because I started sex work early in adulthood, I'm not sure if the lessons I attribute to the job are in fact lessons gained in the usual course of growing up. But judging from the public's reaction when men who are married to great beauties cheat on their wives with less impressive-looking women, a lot of adults remain invested in the notion that a woman's beauty should be protection against suffering and betrayal, and it's not. Nothing is.

Attraction is dependent on so much more than looks alone, though hotness is treated like the determining factor because it's the easiest to package and sell. I'm rarely the best-looking woman in a room, but thanks to sex work, I trust my capacity to charm and seduce, to convince many of those in the room that I am. I know now that when people look at you, they don't see what you look like as much as they see their idea of what you look like, and that idea can be negotiated, improved, revised. Every dimension of a moment—power differentials, circumstance, timing—influences desire, which is capacious but can also be capricious, hyper-specific, and evanescent. Its mutability is a comfort and a curse.

Five or six years into our relationship, Roger told me that on his many flights, while seated early in his preferred position of the first row in first class, he would study the women boarding and ask himself if any were more attractive than I was. "No one ever is," he said. I tried not to roll my eyes over what seemed to be a bold lie and instead appreciate the sentiment behind the words' literal meaning. To him, *better-looking than her* meant *more dear to me than she*. And they weren't.

IN 2014, THE CLIENT from the Boston Symphony incident took me to Las Vegas, where we saw Britney Spears live. The terms of our relationship were garishly obvious as we stood in line beside gay men, groups of girlfriends, and adolescents with chaperone dads. He was thirty-five years my senior and, in heels, I was a foot taller than him. Not that it mattered in Vegas, or anywhere.

We were close to the stage, and when Britney appeared, she

looked puffy and enervated, drugged, which she probably was. It was her dancing that got to me. She performed the familiar motions sluggishly, with so little pleasure that she seemed absent from her body. I knew something about how that felt. In music videos and TV spots from her earlier years, she'd entertained like she was born to do it, a cheetah flashing over the savannah or a gannet dropping like a knife into the sea. None of her imitators could compete with her performance skills no matter how practiced and pretty they were or how they sounded when they sang—her dancing was too special. It wasn't like that anymore. Even that had been taken from her.

We were both aged now. Not old but changed. I'd grown up in the shadow of her sex appeal. I'd envied it, resented it, tried to learn from it, and there I was, being paid for something akin to what she'd sold, accompanied by my client, yes, but in control of myself, attention-catching but not a spectacle, protected by an inner well of deep privacy that was also the source of my power; free from my assignment in two days' time and capable of walking away earlier if I chose. And there she was, owned indefinitely by her conservators, earning money she couldn't touch, consumed ceaselessly like Prometheus, animatronic and erased from herself while I watched. It felt like a moment I'd both engineered and been swept into, a brush with something both beyond me and inside me.

Theoretically, there's no question of who has it better: One of the biggest pop stars of all time, or a prostitute? But there was nothing to envy about her life, and the rush of that knowledge made me turn my head from my date to hide my glassy eyes. Our respective paths seemed utterly strange yet inevitable, parallel and linked, drawn by the same hand. I'd gotten out from under it more than she had, somehow. She was the cautionary tale, the tragedy. I was the success, I think. Or at least I wasn't a pity.

I couldn't have imagined any of this when I lay beneath her poster on Sean's bed, his mouth on my neck, my teeth bright with braces. Sixteen years had passed since then. Britney and I were both in our thirties, but we were living in the same world. "You better work, bitch," she lip-synced below the lights. I stood in the dark, makeup done, dress tight, working.

III

Early into my union with the high school group, one of the girls, Sadie, gave one of the boys—her crush, Tyler—a drunken blow job at a party. He reported back to the rest of the crew that she'd actually blown on him, like she was trying to cool off his boner, and the resultant mockery lasted for months. All of us girls assured Sadie that there was no way for her to have known that the name of the act was so misleading, but she never really lived it down. I wasn't inclined to spontaneously fool around with anyone, drunk or otherwise, but her example chilled me. I'd rather ask for instruction in advance and absolve myself of responsibility for the technique than try to improvise in the moment as if I knew what I was doing. Girls like Britney might be born with intuitive knowledge, but if I wanted to muster up any seductive power, I needed to earn it with humility, planning, determination, and time.

My self-doubt around my desirability was an impediment, but it was offset by the impatience and nosiness of my general disposition. I had that library-kid brand of intrepidness and optimism that begets the conviction that any task is surmountable if you study. I also had a pool of guys I could ask for favors, friend to friend. There was an impersonalness to my request, a clear purpose and conclusion, no room for misunderstandings or lingering expectations. When my father pulled me out of that tent, I hadn't had vaginal sex, but I'd given one boy a hand job and two boys blow jobs at my own initiation and I had every intention to do more of the same.

As a flamboyant, compulsively sexual extrovert and self-appointed sex critic, Tyler was an obvious place to start. Though he had been thoughtless with Sadie, his indiscriminate, overt horniness felt reassuring; anything and anyone turned him on, which I thought would work in my favor. I told him that I wanted him to teach me how to give a hand job, and graciously, he obliged. His erection left no impression on me, though I remember being surprised by the extent of the mess. I also remember him yelling "Get down, Sparky!" repeatedly at his little white dog, who kept jumping on the couch while it happened.

The first blow job took place when I AOL instant messaged a friend from outside the group, a semi-popular guy who went to my school, though we never really acknowledged each other there. Instead we goofed off on instant messenger, and sometimes he called me and played his guitar, making up silly songs over the phone. I told him I'd never done it and wanted to know what it was like. It was a summer weekday, and he drove to my house, where we dry humped behind my closed bedroom door for about ninety seconds, then rushed to have him finish in my mouth. I think my braces made both of us nervous.

The interaction was so quick it hardly counted. My curiosity's itch had not been relieved; it had barely been scratched. More importantly, practice meant *practice*; it meant drilling. I was chiseling out an improved version of myself with the American faith that a better me in the future required concerted effort now, and I was willing to do whatever it took. I thought I'd preempt humiliation by getting these early attempts out of the way, with my ignorance foregrounded and consequently forgiven.

Hand jobs were whatever, a straightforward and minor milestone in the removal of my sexual training wheels, but blow jobs were significant in and of themselves, which may have been the theme of the late '90s. So I tried again in the fall, when I was in a car with Kevin, the most laconic of the boys. It was a spontaneous decision on my part while we were parked on a side street in a residential neighborhood, waiting for someone to come back, probably with alcohol he'd get from another kid. We'd never been alone together before. In fact, we interacted very little, though we were often in the same space.

I was in the driver's seat because Kevin was a year younger and didn't have his license. Also, it was my car. I broke the silence by asking him if he wanted a blow job. "What?" he said, looking over at me. "Okay." He took it out on his own. Again, the event was over almost immediately and did not leave me feeling enlightened. It seemed I barely had to do anything at all, that the whole process just took care of itself; sucking dick was the falling-off-a-log of sex acts. But at least I'd confirmed I could manage it more than once, with different guys, and it wasn't nearly as horrible and disgusting as some girls acted like it would be.

These encounters weren't secrets, nor were they meant to be. I assumed my friends would learn everything, and they did. "Was Kevin's come really bitter?" Justin asked one day when I was at his house. Another girl had told Justin this about Kevin before; privacy was foreign to us all.

"Maybe a little," I responded, having no real point of comparison.

Justin shook his head, threw a hand-size basketball at the net mounted to his rec room wall. "He needs to eat some fucking fruit or something."

The atmosphere of frank disclosure accounts for some of my nonchalance as I progressed through my syllabus. But I was also unfazed by my first real-life erection and its subsequent spill because of my prepubescent immersion in my grandfather's porn, which I'd pore over when my brother and I were left alone in his basement, as we often were. One unforgettable photo shoot took place at a baseball stadium and starred a muscular man with two women in (but mostly out of) team uniform. It stayed with me because of a shot in which the tanned man, kneeling, held up one woman's ass against the shower wall with both his hands as he pressed his face between her thighs. In the foreground, the second woman hid around the corner, a pained look on her glossy face, an expression of exclusion or maybe bliss. (Was she masturbating? I might have missed it.) Everything about the depiction—the drama, their bodies, the position— lifted the lid of my mind.

My favorite spread featured a slim brunette naked on her back between two slight, bearded men with narrow, relaxing erections. They stood on their knees on either end of her, and she had a white wetness on her face, around her mouth. I liked that they looked like cheerful, good-natured people who just happened to be naked. In fact, they looked like friends. "It tastes like milk," the caption of the close-up read. Her tongue was peeking out to lick what wreathed her lips, and she was smiling. I hated drinking milk, but getting just a taste of it wasn't so terrible.

I knew the material was forbidden and therefore bad in some way, but the images made sense despite having no precedent, as if I'd magically acquired a language I'd never heard spoken aloud. I was riveted by what the magazines revealed, not just bare bodies and full-frontal genitals but sex beyond a single male-female coupling, outside of a bed or a discernible romantic relationship.

There must have been pictures in which women looked uncomfortable and bored, and corny shots of ecstatic trances—heads thrown back, eyes closed, lips parted—that may have struck me as inscrutable. Strong emotions are ambiguous when they surface in the face. But if I was upset by anything I saw in those pages, it's long since faded from my memories. What I remember are the women who smiled regular smiles with their eyes open, who seemed as pleasant and engaged as clothed models in a textbook, evincing enjoyment in ways a child could recognize.

The common complaint about *Playboy* pictorials is that the women are plasticized, rendered too airbrushed and uniform to appear real, but my grandfather collected magazines with harder cores than *Playboy*. And in the raunchy pages, sometimes, the impossible occurred. Women had sex and felt good. They were fucked, and fucking didn't harm them.

THE '80S AND '90S were punctuated by multiple nationwide anti-sex hysterias (AIDS, the Satanic Panic, incest stories, and the repressed-memories craze) that seeped into pop culture, personal conversations, news, schools—everything. My seventh-grade sex ed consisted of pictures of advanced venereal diseases and a video of a gruesome hospital birth. Surgeon General Joycelyn Elders became a national laughingstock when she suggested masturbation could be part of the curriculum—I remember watching the *SNL* skits with my father—and swiftly lost her job. In the few romance novels I managed to get my hands on, lovemaking was assaultive and distress was a precursor to, if not a precondition for, the heroine's ravishment. TV shows and movies treated teenage sex as categorically disobedient, secretive, and dangerous, and the hottest girls (who usually, but not always, also acted the sluttiest) got raped or pregnant or both. Even school rumors of acquaintances getting fingered at the movie theater or felt up in a closet sounded rough and abrupt, not like something the girls were into, though I envied them the attention.

I first registered the word "rape" at about eight or nine years old, while watching TV. It was a Sunday, one of my father's custody days, so I asked him what it was, but he wriggled out of telling me. I looked it up in the dictionary when I was alone: *forcible sexual intercourse.* Given context clues, I could discern that rape was disastrous for women, an act that ruined them. But I didn't understand why it was so uniquely awful since, from what I could tell, every sort of sex carried stigma and damage. For virgins, penetration was famously bloody, even if the girl wanted to do it and her partner was her childhood sweetheart. The only way out was through; you had to keep having sex until your body adapted and gave up on signaling you with pain.

And even if the guy loved the girl and the girl loved him, there were always more reasons for her to say no than yes—disease, pregnancy, propriety, religion, her parents. The "yes" column didn't even include sex feeling good to her, just that it would appease the guy, thereby bringing the two of them closer together. Sex was scary, so of course girls would resist and panic when alone with any boy who wanted it. Passion—the very element that made sex sexy—was an amalgam of aggression, intensity, and loss of control, which made intimidation and harm seem foundational to, definitional of, straight sex itself.

Sex was consistently depicted as shameful, life-altering, and traumatic for girls, but none of that was an excuse to avoid it forever. No matter how much intercourse hurt, it was indispensable. Without it, there could be no union, no incentive for a man and woman to meaningfully invest in each other, no method to generate intimacy. I didn't want to be hurt, but I wanted guys to want me and for some of them to love me, so I'd have to have frightening, painful intercourse at least a few times in my life. It was that or die unloved.

WHEN I FOOLED AROUND with boys, I circumvented the prescribed course of events by removing the element of attraction. The situation wasn't volatile or risky because what would happen was made explicit in advance. There was no pressure on me because I was the one initiating, and there was no pain because there was no vaginal penetration—I did stuff to them; they weren't doing anything to me. I didn't even take off my clothes. The guys weren't violent and they weren't attracted to me that way, so arousal wasn't going to turn them into monsters. These were the boys, my boys. My friends. With them, no matter what we did, I'd be safe.

In cutting out pain as I did, though, pleasure went missing, too, at least when it came to partnered acts. With the boys, my priority was information-gathering, not enjoyment. The incidents were engaging and sometimes funny, and nothing left me feeling belittled, but they were unerotic. Our existing friendship extended briefly into a new arena, then retracted back to its usual size. That didn't have the same effect as forming a mutual sexual connection.

From age eleven, I masturbated constantly, using my own vague, imagined scenes of penetration and the lovemaking described in certain books, so I knew that physical stimulation could feel good and that a girl's climax, or at least my own, wasn't elusive. My solo orgasms may have made it easier to think of sexual pleasure and straight sex as two distinct, rarely overlapping phenomena, though I hoped they might merge as I got older.

I didn't masturbate directly to my grandfather's magazines since I looked at them before puberty and I wasn't someplace private. But they were a single shaft of light beamed into an otherwise windowless cell, artifacts that suggested straight sex needn't be all sacrifice and disappointment. The pornographer's lens documented women's penetration unfolding without injury, anguish, terror, or even ambivalence. And these were real people; this was real life. Perhaps sometime, somehow, that would happen to me, too.

THE BOYS REMAINED MY sexual security blanket through college, which I attended close to home. My disastrous devirginizing was performed by one of the boys' older brothers when I was eighteen. I stupidly left that experience to chance, mostly because I was afraid of it, and it was worse than I expected, though at least it was short. We were out on a date, I didn't know him well, and I was so sloppy drunk that while he was getting my underwear off, I began crying about my parents' ancient divorce. I think he stopped before ejaculating, or gave up since I was tight and unhelpful, so even now I'm not sure if it counts as *the* time—though I also don't know who, then or now, I would look to as an arbiter. (A panel of doctors? God?) If there was blood, I didn't see it.

Earlier in the night, I'd met the first man to ever turn my body on from the instant we touched: Jeb, the virginity-taker's friend, who was hot, tall, in his mid-twenties, and hosting the small gathering to which the brother had brought me. The more I drank, the more I flirted with him, until he herded me into his room, pushed my body onto the bed with his, and kissed me. It was my first-ever kiss that felt good, the first one that sparked a bodily reaction unmistakably geared toward orgasm. But I turned him down because I thought it would be too cruel to my date, the guy who wouldn't take my calls after that night. My carefully laid plans with the boys had bought me some time, but ultimately I couldn't outrun the grimly predictable story of the girl rejected by the first boy she joylessly gives it up to. I didn't even like him that much; I just wanted to explore the feeling of being pursued by an older guy. He had nothing to offer me except regret.

For the rest of my college years, I returned to using my friends as a fallback. As I'd feared, vaginal sex was extremely painful, both with the brother whose name I've long forgotten and with Sean, who was his usual obliging self in this as in all things, and who didn't seem less skilled than the average guy. I was never wet or turned on, and after the first instructively hurtful penetration, my body tensed up for subsequent sensations, which then felt even worse. But I wanted to make sure my virginity was really gone, and I wanted to be a woman who had sex, so Sean was called to report for duty. I mercifully let him off the hook after a handful of times. Repetition wasn't yielding improvement. I was already a young freshman, and I graduated college early. I left right away for the city and for grad school.

Yet it was still Sean who accompanied me to our town's most prominent "adult bookstore" to buy the sex toys I needed for webcam work. (I was daunted by the prospect of going alone to such a place and couldn't think of anyone else I wanted with me, so I drove home to visit my mom as a cover for my real local errand.) I picked a semi-realistic, pinkish-beige dildo ribbed with veins and a generic rocket-shaped vibrator, one of those plastic tapered cylinders with the drab functionality of a marital aid from the 1950s. We went back to his house after, but instead of having sex, we lay on his bed while we held the buzzing vibrator against each other's various non-erogenous zones, giggling like we had years before at "The Crow."

THE SAME IMPATIENT ENERGY that guided my sexual forays with the guys drove me to start sex work while at grad school.

A few months into the first semester, I was bored with my classes, disillusioned with academia, and impotently disgusted by one professor's dogged humiliation of my friend, a bedroom-eyed Yale grad whose beauty and quiet intelligence incensed him.

"Why don't you come by my office?" the professor would ask me at the start or the end of class sometimes, or when I ran into him in the hall. He was my advisor and probably the reason my application had been accepted. He emanated a bookish lasciviousness at all times, but I knew he wasn't attracted to me in the way he was attracted to my friend, so I wasn't afraid of him unleashing his sadism on me. I'm sure he would have helped me get published and not expected anything in return besides career-long devotion. But I didn't go to his office. Instead, I went for walks with my friend, during which we both debated dropping out. I wondered when my life of excitement was going to start.

My wildest dreams involved getting paid for being desirable, because payment concretized validation. Becoming desirable was a goal in and of itself, of course, but I wouldn't believe that goal had been achieved until I had the money to prove it. I reasoned that if I were accepted into environments where women were expected to be sexy—if my presence there was tolerated, even if I had a long way to go—there must be a seed of sexiness somewhere in me.

Stripping seemed like a sensible path to actualization, but after I drove to a club downtown, I was too intimidated to go through the doors. I'd never been inside one before, and the building's lack of windows gave off a menacing air. I dialed an escort agency and spoke to a weary-sounding woman who asked, "You get that these guys don't actually want to go out to dinner with you, right?" I did get that, or at least I knew that wasn't all they would want, and in fact I, too, wanted my sex work to be heavy on the sex at that point. I wasn't like the sugar babies who sought men who would shower them with gifts and expensive trips and be content with a mere kiss on the cheek in return. But something about the way the woman spoke made me feel like I wouldn't be safe with her.

I looked at uncategorizable ads that didn't seem sexual but were a little unusual, like a man who advertised $15 an hour for a part-time assistant. When I called him, he described some domestic and office tasks he needed done in his home, then added, "My back gets really sore, so I also like to get massages—can you do that?"

"Oh, I don't know how to do that," I said.

"That's OK, you don't need to go to school for it. Just fifteen minutes or something—a massage, you know? My shoulders?"

After a long silence, I said I didn't think I was what he was looking for.

I thought about trying to be a cocktail waitress—that was racy, wasn't it? It had a vaguely illicit aura, like it could descend into debauchery, and I was still under the impression that in the "real" world, the adult world, men tried to fuck girls in their early twenties regardless of where they met the girls and what the girls were doing, and that those same men were always half prepared to pay for it. But when I called to ask about the job, it sounded like I might not have enough service experience to get hired, and the pay was terrible for such late hours.

Before the end of my first semester, I found a man named Andy on a Canadian matchmaking site that had an option for women to indicate they were seeking sex instead of dating, which wasn't that common on websites back then. The tacit understanding was that such women sought money, too. Andy lived in New Jersey, was married with kids, and tried to impress me by saying he'd invested in a Manhattan restaurant recently visited by Britney Spears. This was 2004, so she was the post-"Toxic," pre–head shaving, still hot-bodied Britney. I thought the name-dropping came off as pathetic and that he wasn't as wealthy as he pretended to be, possibly wasn't wealthy at all. But that didn't stop me from traveling to our date in New York. Even not-rich men find money to spend on women.

He told me our initial meeting would be about making sure we had some chemistry before we did anything physical. But he expected me to meet him inside a hotel room and I didn't protest. I knew there would be sexual contact because sex was the point of our meeting. Yet I was too naive to infer the obvious—that contact would be near-instant. The hotel was derelict, still one of the worst I've ever been in.

"You look better than your pictures," he said after he opened the door. He'd sent me a blurry one of himself in sunglasses, from the chest up. He was in his forties and much heavier than I'd expected. I can't remember if I told him my real name, but I hope not. He apologized for the quality of the hotel and said he'd chosen it for my convenience because it was near Penn Station. His unfamiliarity with the city should have given so much away. He sat next to me on the bed. The conversation portion had concluded. He touched my breasts.

I lay totally still while he wedged his torso between my legs and went down on me. I was not afraid but shocked, stunned into paralysis by a sensation that didn't hurt yet was unbearable. His tongue moving against my labia was meaningless, inexplicable. Its sole purpose seemed to be invasion. He was the first man to put his mouth on me there. I couldn't think of what to do except wait until it stopped.

"You shouldn't just lie there," he said. "You need to make noise or something."

I thought he wanted someone much younger because he liked picturing himself as an initiator or teacher, and that he would get a salacious rush from my bashfulness and the inexperience youth usually entails. He'd made it sound as if he wanted to take his time. It hadn't occurred to me he might want someone like Britney, whose persona telegraphed virtuosity while she professed virginity, like a sorority girl who learned to give legendary head while saving her hymen for marriage. Sex was still pretty new to me; I was certainly not a performer. I hadn't yet trained myself to make encouraging sounds.

The money he gave me at the end was just enough to cover the cost of the round-trip train. *That was awful*, I thought to myself as I waited in Penn Station to go home, giddy with adrenaline, laughing alone as I huddled over my bare legs. *I'm so glad I never have to do it again.*

CAMMING WAS THE SUGGESTION of the man I'd been sleeping with for a few months. Like Andy, he was in his forties and we met through the matchmaking website. But unlike Andy, we spent our first time in public, near Baltimore's National Aquarium, on a Saturday afternoon. He didn't get us a hotel room until the end of our day together and only upon my urging. I wanted to make him spend money on me so I would know he was willing to, and to get a sense of how much he had, which turned out to be very little. In the room, I lay back on the bed, clothed, and he kissed my inner wrist. It made me incredibly wet, and I was so alarmed by it that I sat up and said I had to go. "I've never spent so much on a hotel room in my life," he told me the second time I saw him, but it couldn't have cost more than $300.

His name was Brian, and I wasn't attracted to him, but, as with Sean, I wanted to be sleeping with someone, and this time I was committed to seeing it through, until it became something other than masochism. Guys my own age intimidated me. I worried they'd have higher aesthetic standards and be turned off by my lack of finesse.

Brian knew that I wanted to do some type of sex work because I told him. It wasn't like I felt I owed him the information or needed his permission; I just wanted to talk to someone about it, and I wasn't telling anyone at school. Brian recognized that stripping would have been a disaster for me given my self-consciousness, and he pointed out that it also ran a high risk of being seen by school faculty or students. He suggested I try working on webcam, which I hadn't known was a thing.

I found the cam site through DC's *City Paper*, and my boss there, AJ, was also around forty. He woke up every day in fear of impromptu visits from his mom, who owned the two-story home where he lived and we worked. The rumor was that he'd been arrested twice for selling cocaine to undercover cops, and the webcam studio was his bid at going straight, sort of. (At year's end he offered to commit tax fraud with us models, and not in a smart way.) His mother hated us. When I arrived to work and found her angrily shelving cereal into the kitchen cabinets, I slunk past like a kicked dog.

AJ had two pit bulls, Buffy and Willow. He yelled at them constantly because they barked constantly, and he would also yell at visitors who failed to subdue the chaos. "Pet her!" he'd demand of me in peak agitation while the dogs vaulted over and against each other on his waterbed, and I stood barefoot in a flimsy, overpriced stripper outfit, trying to ask some question about work.

"That's Aaliyah," he said the first time I came by, as he opened the door on a girl in a neon pink lingerie set who bounced on her knees in front of the screen. She was blond and lean and tan and tiny, a nineteen-year-old who looked fourteen. For years I thought she had the most perfect body I'd ever seen. As a sort of audition, I showed AJ my boobs in his basement.

Of all my sex jobs, webcam showcased the worst extreme. Greater harm could be done to me in person, of course, but the anonymity made some men—usually the ones who weren't spending money—vicious, angling to make us cry or otherwise melt down on camera, which wasn't that hard. The only way we earned money was with private shows, and we had to convince men to buy those during free chat. Anyone could log on and say anything to us in free chat while we splayed and bounced and wiggled around on cheap red imitation satin–covered beds with sex toys laid out beside us, and tried to flirt through a stream of abusive text: "I bet you have AIDS." "Ur family hates u." "FAT UGLY WHORE."

AJ wasn't much better. One day he came upstairs to my room and stood in the doorway, looking down at me in my underwear on the mattress on the floor. "What's the matter with you today?" he said. "You look pregnant." I started crying and couldn't stop, even after he apologized and told me he was joking. It was one of the nights when I ended my shift early and went back home in tears, spending more time in the car than I had spent in front of the camera, making less than minimum wage.

After my wretched first week, in a hot bath I tried to fit the peach-colored dildo I'd bought with Sean inside me. The issue hadn't come up yet because I'd sold so few shows, but I'd started to suspect the head was far too fat for me, which it was. I couldn't force it inside. Selling sex is easy. But not that easy. I stared at a skinny ribbon of blood wavering in the water and wondered what I thought I was doing and when I would get better at it.

Despite being such a tragic failure in those early days, I didn't give up. Quitting felt like it would mean conceding that I'd never be sexy. This was the moment when I either had to learn how to be hot or settle for being just as I was, and I wasn't willing to do that. I had so much to figure out, including how to have sex without excruciating pain. Regardless of the promising wrist kiss in the hotel and Brian's general competence, penetrative sex with him was not any better than it had been with the dildo, Sean, or the other guy—until the day when I truly paid attention to my body, communicated with Brian about the pace, and willed myself to relax. Then, suddenly, it wasn't.

"It didn't hurt!" I told Brian afterward, elated. I felt like I'd discovered a superpower. He asked how I'd done it, and I answered, "Determination without frustration." It became my mantra for that period of my life.

DURING SPRING BREAK FROM my master's program, I reunited with Sean and Justin when I went home for a family visit. Sean told me he jerked off to memories of our sex and asked me if it was wrong of him to do that. He was very drunk, the only sort of drunk he got, and couldn't have been serious. Our dry, awkward sex? With me, the anti-Britney, who'd felt like she was being stabbed in the vagina with a knife still in its sheath? I wasn't even convinced he'd gotten off during it. Those times seemed so far in the past. My few months on webcam had made me a new woman.

That same night, Justin, who knew about my job on cam, told me I looked "great . . . like, amazing" and asked to see my breasts while we were in the car. I told him no. He offered me $50, and I turned him down, shocked, laughing, not angry that he'd offered but sad to think that he believed money would get me to say yes. I loved him so much. Truly, I loved him the most, more than Noah or Sean, more than almost anyone. If he really wanted something from me—anything—if he needed it, I would give it to him. But this curiosity was transitory and idle, meaningless. He was impulsive and drunk. "Give me a little kiss," he mumbled, and I did. "Give me another one," he said, and I told him I had to go.

I wondered later where my line was, and why. Wasn't it nicer for me to do sexual things with my friends, people I trusted and cared about, than with strangers? Hadn't that been my operating assumption for years? I owed the boys a lot, and it was hard to think of any request I could make of them that they would refuse me—though it was also hard to imagine me asking for something they wouldn't want to give. I was more confident since I'd start working, a lot more confident, but part of that came from being in the city, surrounded by people I didn't know and didn't necessarily care about. The old self-consciousness was still there. If Justin thought my boobs looked weird, he might not announce it to a roomful of people, but the knowledge would still be in his head. Some part of me worried it would make him love me less or change the dynamic between us in some other way. I couldn't risk it, not with him.

That fear was unfair, immature, and before I'd left for grad school, it had been almost fully snuffed out by years of reassurance as to the boys' acceptance. *It's great that I have people I can be really comfortable with*, I wrote in my college journal, using the word "people" but meaning "boys." I'd just gotten home from rolling around with one of the other guys in his bed after his parents fed me dinner. That night, I was trying to decide if I should have sex with him, and I told him as much; we discussed it. He'd once asked if I wanted to hold his penis while he peed, and I said no and made fun of him for asking, but I should have said yes. I wish I had. It was such an inspired impulse. If he'd taken my virginity, he would have done it thoughtfully and with care. *Even though we were being fairly intimate, and we talked about sex, I'm not going to feel weird around him the next time I see him*, I wrote. *It's like the physical stuff doesn't matter because we know each other so well.*

The boys extended to me what the artist Hannah Black calls

"the collegiate, unpretentious sexual warmth" characteristic of gay men that's usually withheld between straight men and women. And in doing so, they invited me inside a sort of hedonistic Eden, a space of inclusion and innocence that existed alongside feral vulgarity. How miraculous that I'd been a part of that. Their generosity gave me something far more precious than sexual pleasure, and I would yearn to feel it again for the rest of my life.

IN THE WHOLE OF my career, I've only worked one bachelor party. The best man, Josh, found my listing in the fetish section of an advertising site and asked if I'd make an hour-long appearance for eight "professional-type" guys who—he promised—would act as a respectful audience for my humiliation and abuse of the groom. He cited the Nine Inch Nails music video for "Sin" as potential inspiration. The video includes scenes of genital piercings, a man wearing a strap-on, someone being spun around in an aerotrim, and a topless woman holding a small dog. It was useless as far as practical guidance, but the video convinced me that Josh was sort of a dork, like so many people into BDSM are, and that made me trust him more.

After further discussion, we settled on a scenario. I'd knock on their suite's door and pretend to be a fellow hotel guest who was mad about the noise, then invite myself in once that I saw they were having a party. I wore a trench coat, black lingerie, and heeled boots. I brought along a strap-on, clothespins, a crop, and a paddle. I was supposed to boss around the groom, embarrass him, hit him, and then do something more overtly arousing, like play with his nipples and put my cleavage in his face. Josh repeatedly promised that he'd be sober so he could act as de facto bodyguard for me and stressed that he didn't want his life ruined by some other guy acting stupid. I was more concerned with doing a good job than I was walking into danger. I wasn't a real stripper, so I felt like a fraud, and I didn't want to disappoint.

The men were in high spirits when I arrived, rowdy in the best way. They roared and cheered over my every move; they were a performer's dream. No one touched me except the groom and only when I told him to. They were current and former military men, and while I have no sentimental notions about the armed forces, they were perfect gentlemen. I had the time of my life.

After making a spectacle of the groom for about forty-five minutes, Josh and I took him into one of the bedrooms and shut the door. I hadn't picked up on something in the "Sin" video that in retrospect was glaringly obvious, which is that it features many shots of two men caressing each other. I wasn't offering full service then, just hand jobs, so I sat on the groom's right side and jerked him while Josh lay on his left side and talked his friend off. This was less fun, because it was so clear that I was merely a proxy and buffer as opposed to a real participant. I was interfering with something between them even as I facilitated it, but it wasn't my place to say so or stop. Still, the ability to be a voyeur of other people's most personal lives was one of the job's best perks.

When I stepped back out into the hotel hall with my adrenaline pumping and my bag full of tips, I felt like I'd peaked. *This* was what I was really meant to do, I thought. This was the perfect booking, the best it would ever get. I'd experienced magical one-on-one sessions at work, but those encounters tended to be slightly unreal, like a spell, as if they took place in a fleeting universe of pure romantic fantasy that only two people could enter. I left the party with the sense of having sunk deliciously down into the pleasures of the actual world rather than spinning up and out above them, and it inspired a wild greed in me, not for money but for more of that experience.

Once I came down from the high, I knew I wouldn't make more doing events than I made with fetish and body rub sessions, and changing my business model when it was going so well seemed unwise. Maybe if I'd followed through with the career pivot, I'd have discovered that bachelor parties really were my calling. But if extraordinary moments were so easy to re-create, they wouldn't be extraordinary.

That night wasn't a perfect replica of my nights with the boys, but it approximated them. I was welcomed into a zone of masculine joy and fellowship, embraced by the occupants, and made delirious by their exuberance. There was the wholesome reception of sex, too, its frictionless presence among platonic laughter and celebration, no judgment or shame within that circle of grace. I had so much fun. I think they all had so much fun. But within the celebration was also a goodbye. Their opportunities to do something like this were disappearing. They were married or marrying; they had kids or were planning for them; they didn't live in the same cities. I would never again enter their hedonistic Eden, but they probably wouldn't either.

IV

In-person sex work started for me in the fall of 2005. I'd kept working on webcam since I finished grad school, but I was getting tired of it, so I turned to the *City Paper* ads again, the same place where I'd found AJ's studio.

The first number I called was an arms dealer ("government contractor") looking for beautiful women to dress "like ladies" and entertain their clients, which sounded risky and weird. The second led to an awkward exchange with a woman who offended me when she speculated that cam work must not pay well. "I made forty-two thousand dollars last year," I corrected her haughtily. "And I'll probably make seventy thousand dollars this year." She was skeptical of those figures and of me as a whole—I'd irritated her when I said something narc-sounding like, "I know you can't tell me what *really* happens in a session, but can you give me some idea?" Her service was listed as "private viewings," which sounded like what I was already doing online—getting naked, masturbating, talking dirty. When we met at a bland café in Crystal City, she explained that massage without a license was illegal in Virginia, where the incall was located, which necessitated the ambiguous name. "They mostly just want to touch your boobs," she told me when I asked again for a better idea of what clients would expect.

Sherri, the proprietor of the agency, was a petite white brunette in her thirties with a five-year-old son whom I never met and she rarely mentioned. Her split of the $180 hourly rate was slightly in favor of the girl instead of the house ($95 for me, $85 for her), which was unheard of. We spoke on the phone frequently once I came on board, but I didn't see her much after our first meeting. She left face time to her assistant, Tina, a chubby girl in her early twenties who answered calls and ate snacks in the living room whenever she wasn't off running mysterious errands. Tina was so blasé and placid that she bordered on bovine. She once told me to use a tampon when I tried to call out for the day because I had a yeast infection too noticeable to work through, then suggested that the guys would like the discharge because they'd just assume I was turned on. Depressingly, she was probably right.

Yeast infections were a fixture of my life during this time, along with my first bout of jock itch, because Sherri's line about the guys just wanting to touch boobs was a huge lie. Clients, as it turned out, wanted everything, especially to eat me out. I let them get away with too much because I was young and inexperienced and working at the incall was exhilarating. I fell in love with the job completely: the pageant of characters, the cash, the sex. I worked like I was trying to make partner, baffling Sherri with how often I requested to be put on the schedule. Most of the women only wanted a day or two per week, but I'd do four or five. In a way, it was like working for the government, since local contractors, many of whom were current or former military, referred each other to the agency and pulled their cash from accounts fat with taxpayer funds.

Rhetoric against sex work relies heavily on the vision of women "servicing" men back-to-back to trigger disgust and revulsion, but I loved seeing multiple people in one afternoon. Being booked with no breaks made the time fly and the money stack up. Also, I was practically in heat for the duration of my twenties and I hadn't had the opportunity to sample so many men in the flesh. Excluding my remote webcam customers, I'd barely had any partners, so the breadth of this sudden variety was dizzying. Before the incall I hadn't experienced the sort of wordless chemistry that hits like a speedball, hijacking the body with its imperative. One of the first times I fucked a client, it happened in a breath-stealing flash. There was no negotiation about his paying more. There was no condom because I didn't have them with me—I wasn't "supposed" to be having penetrative sex, so I didn't prepare for it—and if he brought one with him, he didn't say so. We saw each other, and I needed him inside me. He got inside me. That was the fun of the incall. If I wanted to do something, I did it. I felt powerful.

Work turned me on even when I wasn't at work—the idea of it, the fact of it, sat like a vibrating egg in the back of my mind. And the men I met there, at least some of the men, a good number of men, got me off in spite of themselves. I could find their behavior gross or their bodies unappealing, but they might have a touch that rushed me to the edge, or they arrived at a fortuitous moment, on the tail of a client who left me aching. Or my hormones were flaring up that day, or the client was genuinely sexy, or sometimes it was several of those things at once. I think I scared off at least one man when my desire made me so savage that I straddled him on the bed and rubbed myself against the wide side of his erection until I came. As I stood at the door telling him goodbye, I felt a thick rivulet of period blood release down my inner thigh and locked my eyes on his to keep his gaze from moving down. I hadn't realized it was that time.

My behavior could be outrageous and would seem especially so to anyone who's never lost themselves in the crevasse of their arousal before, or who banishes the memory from their mind once they have. I made fun of clients who told me similar stories about other women they'd paid to be with: college girls who spontaneously started sucking their dick or met them for free outside of work. I dismissed these tales as delusional fantasies and crudely fashioned gambits to get me to do something they wanted me to do, or to do it for free, which didn't take much maneuvering if they caught me at the right time. My rates made no sense because they were set by mood and caprice: $100 extra to give a blow job, $100 tip to have vaginal sex with some clients, no tip at all for others. It was lawless. One regular gave me $100 extra no matter what we did, including anal, which bothered me some, but mostly he just followed my lead when it came to how we spent our time. As for adjusting the rate based on the presence or absence of a condom, that was well beyond me then. It didn't take me too long to become stricter and more financially minded. But in those first few months, I exercised no restraint or common sense.

I wasn't such an anomaly. One escort I knew, an absolutely stunning blonde, was a licensed massage therapist who got into the work when one of her clients asked to pay more for a happy ending. At the time, she was an Evangelical Christian who'd only had sex with her husband, but once she crossed the threshold, she turned into a fiend, and soon her massage clientele was comprised exclusively of men she got off in some form or another. She divorced her husband, quit offering sex-free massage, and put up a website to properly pursue full service full time. She charged much less than she could have because she liked being high volume and, in her resilient sweetness, felt like $300 an hour was already a lot.

Though my escort friends and I were scornful of clients who imagined our work as purely pleasurable, it could be a blast. Women with straight jobs who started moonlighting as strippers or call girls often left the white-collar world to spend more time at their sex job because it paid more, offered more control over working conditions, and entailed less harassment. I took these escorts' word for it that their clients treated them better than customers and bosses in other contexts. So many of them said so, it couldn't have been just a few flukes. And all of us agreed that clients treated us better—exponentially better—than most of the men we fucked for free.

BECAUSE OF MY ENTHUSIASM and resultant lax boundaries at Sherri's incall, I never wanted for customers, and so I black-listed with abandon. If a guy was creepy, rough, obnoxious, or just unpleasant and didn't tip enough to make tolerating him worth it, I told Sherri I didn't want to see him again, and she was supposed to honor that. Yet some of those men showed up at my door anyway. "I didn't know you meant *that* David," she would say afterward, irritated, semi-apologetic at best. It seemed she only kept track of guys by their first names and phone numbers, maybe sometimes a last initial, and the lack of variation was astounding. (I wouldn't be sur-prised if 40 percent of my clients have been named John and another 20 percent Mike or Steve.)

But Sherri was shrewd, and I think she only pretended to for-get, which—in addition to the considerable financial incentive—was why I left her to start working on my own. I wanted more control over who I saw and what those people expected because the variety at Sherri's was unsustainably demanding. Through experience, gossip shared by clients, and help from my wiser friend Emily, I eventually learned that some girls kept their underwear on for the whole session or only gave hand jobs, no matter if they were naked or mostly clothed, or if the client offered them money for more. At Sherri's, no one ever told me what, exactly, the clients I saw were paying for. Overearnest as I was, this meant I didn't know what they were allowed to expect of me, and so I didn't know how to react when they started fingering me or going down on me.

Just because I enjoyed sex with some clients or might spend the whole day turned on didn't mean I wanted to do everything with everyone. Most men were terrible at fingering, and it didn't matter how cute they were or how aroused I was: I hated it when they went down on me. But I didn't know how to stop it. Squirming away or closing my legs didn't work. There was no point in telling clients I was on my period or had a yeast infection even when I was or did because they didn't care. Lots of agency regulars asked for the new girl, or would say yes without seeing pictures, because odds were good that she'd be easy to pressure, intimidate, and confuse. Men who booked women for a body rub tended to be pushy in general, and the more forbidden acts there were, the more they had to be pushy about. These were men who wanted intercourse and oral but didn't want to pay the going rate, nor did they want to use any protection, and they didn't want to see someone fully willing; they wanted to coax or violate or both at once. It was exhausting.

After I left Sherri's in 2006, I offered a service more tailored to what I liked and felt I was best at. My sessions combined the nebulous aspect of private viewing with an emphasis on fetishes, and I only advertised under body rub and BDSM categories, not escort. I met better clients and kept some of my old ones once I went solo, but even with my own marketing and screening, the same frustrations arose. The path of least resistance would always be giving in, but it was more complicated now because the men were often regulars convinced that they'd formed deep emotional connections with me—or maybe that was part of the manipulation. Regardless, it was one thing to spend forty minutes grappling with an agency guy I might never see again and another to try to rhetorically dissuade the guy who booked me every week for two hours of make-believing that we were in love. By this time, I also saw sex in starker economic terms. If any client wanted to fuck me so bad, he should pay for it, but it would ruin the fantasy if, in the moment, I asked how much extra cash he'd brought.

It became clear that working full service—allowing blow jobs and vaginal sex—would be easier and safer as well as more lucrative. I shifted to straight-up escorting and emailed my regulars to let them know I was offering something new that I'd love to share with them, if they were interested. The headaches went away. The more I charged and the fewer explicit boundaries I put up, the less conniving and physically demanding my clients were. Some still tried to forgo protection, but they were a dwindling minority. Unlike the common prostitute and the common slut, the classy prostitute—as indicated by her price point—deserves to have her laws obeyed, from the screening requirements to the interpersonal conduct. (The men I hooked up with recreationally, who tended to be younger and far less monied than my escorting clients, and who had no idea about my hourly rate, were as awful about condoms as the body rub gang.)

Because condom use has become culturally correlated with morality—good, responsible people use condoms and bad, dirty ones don't—I feel acutely aware that some people would shame me for having unprotected sex at work and that my naivety would be no defense against their scorn. I also know those people are unlikely to direct the same condemnation at the married, middle-aged men who were my partners in transgression, the ones who paid for access to my body. Maybe I was the only person they did that with. Maybe it was just the one time. Maybe there really was no sex at all, ever, with their spouses. But I marvel at those men and the expanse of their selfishness. My decisions reflected my newness in that world; I was an amateur. But they acted with experience. They were the old pros.

My LIBIDO WAS LESS tyrannical by the time I left Sherri's, but once I struck out on my own, my enjoyment of the work deepened. I continued to meet people whom I'd never spend time with in my normal life, men with unusual hobby jobs and inscrutable family wealth, men who worked for the IMF and the World Bank, an Oscar-winning celebrity. I liked having—being—their secret. And I was taking in so much cash, which helped me tolerate the more obnoxious or boring dates.

When I'd left home for grad school, it was with the resolution to stop being a burden on my mother, who, I'd learned, had virtually no financial assistance from my dad while I was growing up. (He hadn't even paid his meager court-mandated child support, though he claimed me as a dependent on his taxes.) Because I had a full scholarship, my living costs were modest, and webcam work covered them amply.

After I completed my master's, I moved in with Brian, the older man I'd started dating near the start of my program. He'd taken a job in DC, and—I learned about a year into cohabitation—handled "our" finances by having me pay two-thirds of the rent, all the utilities, and at least half the bill when he took me out to dinner. The incall money helped me get out of that situation; I replaced funds faster than he could drain them. I moved into an English basement that was all mine, took time off for travel, then came back ready to hustle in earnest. This era, 2008 into 2009, marked my professionalization. I threw myself into marketing, made smart decisions about my steadily increasing rate structure, and amassed a pool of devoted regulars. Escorting became my career.

To stack cash is as hypnotizing as every song and movie claims. Watching an electronic bank balance go up is satisfying, but nothing compares to holding money, banding it, piling it into a safe. My boyfriend after Brian bought me a cash-counting machine that I dismissed as gratuitous, but it quickly became indispensable. Nothing necessitated my working as much as I did; I wasn't in debt or dire financial straits, and my most expensive habit was clothes shopping, which never outpaced what I brought in. But there was so much money to be made, why shouldn't I make it? I relished being so accomplished. It didn't just feel like being good at a job. It felt like being good at being a woman.

IT'S HARD TO KEEP your ego in check when you have dozens or hundreds or thousands of men kissing your ass, but most sex workers retain (or regain) perspective if they stay in the industry for a few years. Usually that's because they've caught on to the impersonal mechanisms of success, but it also helps that displays of modesty come easy when you're in high demand. "I am not a supermodel—far from it," wrote Natalie McLennan about her mid-2000s stint as the self-proclaimed highest-paid escort in New York. "My secret was I made guys want to hang out with me."

McLennan worked a lot with Ashley Dupré, a fact she plays up from the start of her book, *The Price: My Rise and Fall as Natalia, New York's #1 Escort*. Ashley is described as young and guileless, not a savvy schemer like McLennan; her secret is that she has "the glow," and "a near-perfect body" including a "beautiful coochie" that would make her the city's next escort phenomenon. However accurate that may be, whatever Ashley achieved before the Spitzer scandal, her magic was not effective on Roger, at least not effective enough to get him to book another date. I wonder if Natalie was the nameless partner in his infamous Time to Eat the Pussy threesome, the one who didn't make enough of an impression to warrant mention. It feels obvious to me that looks don't matter as much as outsiders might think, but I'm not sure personality matters so much either.

I tend to think of myself as having been excellent at my job in my heyday, and I definitely was, sometimes. When I liked the work, I was sweet, easily aroused, sexually attentive. With clients who enjoyed sparring and Old Hollywood–style banter, I was bright and playful. With clients who needed solace, I was soothing and gentle. But there were other times, during daylong or multiday dates, when I was a nightmare: aloof, enervated, contemptuous, frigid. I think back on my behavior with some clients, the mild-mannered ones whose only offense was booking me at a time when I was burned out or in a bad mood, and I feel ashamed. Yet often an expensive, bratty weekend didn't dissuade them from hiring me again.

I acquired and used real skills, sexual and otherwise, but whatever efforts I made were met more than halfway by clients' loneliness and yearning and how they responded to youth. A craving for connection will fulfill itself by creating an appropriate object. I pared myself down for that fantasy and polished what was left behind, to accommodate whatever the client would bring to and place upon me. In truth, I wasn't the woman. I was the pedestal.

MY PARENTS SEPARATED WHEN I was so young that I have no recollection of them as a couple, but I do remember some of the early years after their divorce. Once my father moved into a new house, my brother and I went there every other weeknight for dinner. There, my dad would excuse my brother from the table after he'd finished but keep me there so he could talk to me about his failed relationship with my mom. I can't say what thought process convinces a man it's right to expound to a seven-year-old about the affair (his own) that ensured the end of his marriage, and his resentment toward her mother, his ex-wife. But I imagine he told himself he needed to make me privy to parts of his version of the story lest my mother be the only one pouring poison in my ear. (She wasn't.) Men are in the habit of telling themselves that girls are, by some queer feat of biology, "mature for their age," and, in my experience, the men who say that are unable to recognize a sensitive situation as such—perhaps because for them, the situation is not emotionally fraught and confusing but cathartic and controlled.

My dominant memory of those nights with my father is how much I wished he didn't make me do it, of trailing a fork over my dirty plate and wondering when I would be released to watch TV with my brother. I knew the scene was wrong. Adults were not supposed to treat children this way, were not supposed to talk to them like this. It felt strange and bad, not least of all because I couldn't speak freely. My dad sometimes asked me what I thought of whatever he'd just said—about something my mom had done, or the odds of her forgiving him—and I knew better than to answer with what he didn't want to hear, so I'd plead ignorance or deflect.

I was the older child, and that may have played a role in my selection, but it seems to me that my father did what he did because I was female. If he needed care, I should have been the one to provide it because regardless of age, women are designated emotional custodians. He sought reassurance, not connection, in my pliability. His authority exerted pressure to make me stay put and listen, and I saw my father's weakness in those moments—his vulnerability, his dishonesty, and his delusions. I didn't agree that he was a victim of my mother's irrationality or selfishness, but I still felt sorry for him because I loved him. I didn't want him to be in pain, and he seemed to believe I could help alleviate that pain. So his authority acted in concert with my conscience.

More than anything else in my life, I think, those early exercises in diplomacy and male validation prepared me for work as an escort. I've since sat quietly at hundreds of tables during an older man's uninterrupted holding forth, and I became good at lying with my intermittent responses. It took some cleverness, but it wasn't hard. Draining, but not hard. On the contrary, it was second nature, an acquired behavior fully integrated into my manner of being. I know many women have this mollifying ability, and many of us learned it by interacting with our fathers. It turns us into effective emotional-support animals for the rest of our lives—if not sex workers, then dutiful wives and girlfriends and subordinates. In *SCUM Manifesto*, Valerie Solanas writes that fathering is "the male's major opportunity to control and manipulate," and so produces "daddy's girls" who are "passive, adaptable, respectful," patiently permitting him "to impose his hideously dull chatter on her."

Men are notoriously bad at asking questions, and even Roger, who professed to find me so captivating, rarely asked me about myself. That could be attributed to his respect for my boundaries, but when I chose to share what I thought was a relevant anecdote or cute personal story, it was often as if I hadn't spoken at all. When the only other occupant in a room chooses not to acknowledge what you've said, the resulting silence is a rebuke. I had, apparently, participated out of turn.

It's funny that what seemed to be the best feature of my service was also held against me. Clients liked that I was "mysterious." It made them feel good about themselves, like they had a taste for depth and complexity, without impeding who they wanted me to be. But some complained that I was evasive and impossible to get information from. People I think of as friends occasionally say the same, which surprises me. At work, I was slippery because that was how I wanted to be, but in my personal life, I feel like I have nothing to hide and am happy to share. Yet prevarication is my default setting.

I think it became so entrenched in my adult life because dissembling wasn't just a selling tactic. First and foremost, it was a safety precaution. As careless as I sometimes was with my body, I was instinctually much more protective of my private life: details about where I lived and with whom I spent time but also my truest thoughts, plans, values. I never wanted to share what mattered most to me with clients. Why would I? It was unprofessional and bad for business. (I believed oversharers set off alarms in any client worth having.) But mainly, I didn't trust them. Too many men amassed escorts' secrets like arcade tickets, to be spent on fulfilling an impulsive desire, or handed off to someone else when they got bored with playing, or just dropped and trampled when the thrill of receipt was gone.

HOBBYISTS, AS THE MOST prolific men on sex worker review boards called themselves, developed an appetite for sheer repetition. They became compulsive collectors, completionists of the escort world, driven less by sincere enthusiasm than some notion of dominion. During appointments, they were greedy and stingy, emotionally absent—qualities they abhorred in women they hired. Worse, they were vengeful, because they believed they had a right to control every hooker's success and to access her whenever they wanted. They didn't hesitate to trash a girl who wouldn't see them again or who raised her rates, and they tacitly and explicitly threatened as much when necessary. The most popular site, The Erotic Review, fostered this in its users through its functionality and conventions.

Not every guy wrote reviews like that, and for some escorts, reviews were integral to their marketing. But the hobbyist mentality was regrettably prominent even among men who didn't write reviews. Just reading the site's listings or looking at the message board might be enough exposure for someone to adopt it. There were drop-down fields on every woman's profile where clients were supposed to indicate her body type ("curvy," "slim," "a few extra pounds"), the quality of her breasts ("perky," "youthful," "super nice"), and estimate her age, height, weight, cup size. Naturally, attractiveness and performance were summed up by a number rating between one and ten. Expectations were categorized with repulsive lingo condensed to somehow even more repulsive acronyms: MSOG (multiple shots on goal, meaning you'd be given more than one orgasm); DATY (dinner at the Y, which meant eating pussy); DFK (deep French kissing); and so on. The worst of them expected sloppy, tongue-heavy making out ("she LOVES to kiss," they'd write); a DTBBBJN-QNS (deep-throat bareback blow job no quit no spit); and at least one round of multi-position vaginal sex, all performed by a gorgeous, effusive, inexhaustibly orgasmic young woman whose rates hewed to her city's average.

Roger had an account on The Erotic Review and wrote reviews when a woman asked him to. When together, we followed the TER formula to some extent—the order is textbook straight sex, paid or unpaid—but he wasn't an aggressive kisser and rarely wanted sex to last more than fifteen or twenty minutes from start to finish. I mimicked enjoyment, but he didn't try to force my orgasms, and they didn't occur naturally, which was fine by me. After I started working for myself, I realized I didn't like coming at work. It was too private, and I hated turning it into a gimmick delivered on demand as if I were a captive animal doing tricks. Being able to determine when and how and if I came felt like an important indicator of my control over the encounter as a whole.

Moreover, I worried real orgasms would throw my faking into relief, thereby setting the bar too high for future sessions, though eventually I learned clients found my true orgasms less satisfying than the fake ones. It's not fair to say their unwitting preference was proof that they didn't care about my actual pleasure. They just cared about their own more, and my climax mattered not because of how good it would feel to me but because of how good it would feel to them.

I was grateful for the men who let me get away with disliking the sex, or who at the very least didn't belabor my pleasure and the degree to which it was or wasn't real. It was tactful and mature of them, like someone tipping their server well even when the server doesn't smile. I hated the men who insisted on trying to manipulate my genitals to climax, who badgered me to teach them how to get me off, like we were a couple trying to overcome intimacy issues. They seemed convinced the matter was a technical problem, not the normal outcome of a lack of desire and attraction. Their approach was so much more presumptuous and invasive than that of the guys who allowed me my displeasure.

One of the most annoying aspects of the job was the lead-up to and delivery of the fake orgasm. I thought clients were entitled to expect it, especially given what I charged, but it was still a big source of resentment. There were incidents when I couldn't bring myself to do it at all, and on especially spiteful occasions, when a client wouldn't stop going down on me, I'd channel my anger into faking the most absurd orgasm I possibly could, flopping and vocalizing like I was auditioning for the role of Electrocuted Woman in a slapstick comedy and not even earning the part. I don't know if they bought it, but their buying it wasn't really the point. Afterward, I'd turn my head and press my face into my arm as if I were collecting myself, though I was checking the bedside clock. I did that a lot with the more modestly faked ones, too.

Roger sometimes prompted me to show him how I masturbated or asked me to direct him on my body, but these occasions were few. I don't recall ever enjoying our sex, because it was devoid of eroticism and (on my end) physical attraction. But at least under normal circumstances it didn't take too long and wasn't physically grueling. I made the right noises and tried to move in a convincing manner. I think he believed that I liked it even if he wasn't under the illusion that I came.

He didn't come much either. In fact, for most of our relationship, Roger didn't orgasm with me. When it first started— or stopped—he didn't seem surprised. He told me he had a long-standing problem coming with women he respected too much. He was self-conscious, eager to impress, and his brain couldn't reconcile making a good impression with ejaculating. That was why he'd seen so many different escorts before me, I realized; he could come with them once and not face them again. Between us, without the climax, he'd simply stop when he'd had enough and hug me to his chest, giving a sigh of ostensible contentment. Closeness was the goal, and that was easy to achieve. "Tell me you're happy to see me," he'd say, and I would.

IT'S COMMON FOR CLIENTS to fall in love with their sex workers. Infatuation can be about the worker, kind of, who she really is and how she behaves. But the rush and weight of feeling come from the container of the interaction. The situation is compelling—its taboo, the associated risks, the way it distills sex—and it crystalizes sex into a unit so it can be served up like a line of cocaine. As is true with a lot of drugs, the high isn't just about the product but the drama of arranging and indulging in it. There are secret accounts and second phones, lies about business obligations and furtive visits to the ATM.

If you market well enough, your reputation can do a lot of the work. No one likes to feel that they've wasted time and money or that they have bad taste or are easily duped. Circumstances primed clients to feel that they were with an irresistible woman, a woman most men yearned to be with and never would. There's also curiosity and the fear of missing out. When a woman charges a lot and seems to be working a lot, it follows that there's a reason for her success—she's exceptionally beautiful or a sexual expert or both. Clients want to find out for themselves. They don't want to pass up the opportunity to meet someone extraordinary. Sex workers are hopelessly fascinated by sex workers, too. They'll arrange threesomes to meet a girl they're curious about, stalk each other's personal social media, gossip about colleagues on message boards. They can pretend it's professional competition or due diligence, but it's not.

When I worked on webcam, Aaliyah, one of the other women at my studio, told me she kept our site open in the background of her screen to watch girls in free chat during her shift. I tried her tactic in case it would improve my salesmanship, but it didn't. It plunged me into a miasma of jealousy, envy, and uncertainty.

The girls were so pretty, or not that pretty but still magnetic, and sometimes so bitchy. If I typed in a nice comment and they didn't acknowledge it, I tried again. If they ignored me several times, I became enraged. If a girl was in private for a long time, the deprivation was unacceptable, like a targeted insult.

Being attracted to the models, being interested in them, somehow felt like being manipulated and mistreated. Seeing a woman on a screen suggests there's something special about her, and as a viewer you want to crack open the special thing and poke around inside, squeeze and taste the center. It didn't matter that I was on-screen, too, or that I knew how easy it was to get there. Their self-presentation felt like a provocation. The physical nearness of in-person work defangs this, dilutes the rage. But sometimes, it roots the reaction even deeper down in a client's psyche, where it takes on a cast of profundity.

In Yasunari Kawabata's "House of the Sleeping Beauties," a sixty-year-old man pays to spend the occasional night sleeping next to a drugged, naked woman in her teens. Though he never penetrates a girl nor orgasms at the house, the man imagines the beauties are "giving everything over to him," then that they are witches casting a spell, giving away nothing at all. "Woman is infinite," he thinks, believing his lack of perception, his commitment to preventing their engagement, indicates the presence of a uniquely female opacity.

"When it comes down to it, every escort is just some girl," my friend Lily said once when I was feeling angsty about a competitor, and she was right. But they seem like so much more. It's the contrast between what is and isn't revealed, the subconscious awareness of what's being withheld and what's being offered, the soul's intolerable ungraspability combined with the body's availability, and the intimation that, because of the rarefied circumstances, this soul is uncommon and wild. It's so easy for a man to fall in love with a girl, any girl, who's been removed from herself—or to imagine he's in love, anyway. To be stoked to extremes by the presence of a form and the absence of a her.

Roger told me more than once that when I left him, he looked at the pictures on my website to remind himself that I was real. People like looking at those they care about, or anyone they find beautiful. But what information could an image give him that would confirm who he imagined me to be? A girl can be a fragment in the mind of a man, but she doesn't exist (solely) in the man's mind. She exists in the world, where the man looks at her in silence and savors his refusal to comprehend what he sees.

WHEN I STARTED SEX work, I was afraid of what men as a violent and volatile class could do, might do, were rumored to habitually do, but I hadn't—still haven't—experienced anything near to the worst of it. I had trouble relating to working women who spilled over with messy rage, the sort who stole cash from clients' wallets or homes and fantasized about stabbing a guy while fucking him. "We'd tell their wives," Michelle Tea wrote about her time selling sex. "Make fun of what they'd wanted, make sure they understood we had not enjoyed it. Ask them to please stop [hiring] prostitutes." When one client wrote a bad check to a friend of mine, she enlisted her social circle to enact an elaborate revenge—or justice—involving a camera, the man's father, and the threat of violence. It worked; she got her money. But her measures alarmed me.

I never had to do anything like that, and I don't know that I'd have been able to. Any drama is too much drama; I require all my dealings to be neat. My most combative moments involved threatening to out a man who antagonized me, but I only resorted to that after suffering through months of invasive obsession. The offender posted pictures of my face on local message boards to ask for information about where I lived and encourage anyone who recognized me to contact the police or the FBI. "She may be someone you know or even a coworker with a double life," he wrote in one of many listings, transparently optimistic, hoping for me to have a straight job he could use as a weapon to foreclose my future by wrecking my present. He was a former military serviceman, current military contractor. He had two children. I met him before I learned to listen to my instincts, which took years to do. He was one of the least attractive people I'd ever been with, and I mistook my unease for shallowness.

When I hired a lawyer to communicate on my behalf through

the anonymous email addresses the military man attached to his posts, he told the lawyer he would stop if I quit escorting and agreed to start seeing a therapist of his choosing. Instead, the harassment ended after I said I would tell his wife and colleagues, which might be evidence that my friend's guerrilla method of dealing with bad clients is the smarter and quicker way.

"My belief that there was something that brought us together is unwavering," he wrote in one of his last emails to me under his own name, when he seemed to think my reluctance to see him again had to do with my preparation to stop sex work altogether, probably so I could start one of those office jobs I'd heard so much about. "And I will say that without a doubt I feel that there indeed was a purpose behind it, which I'm now beginning to understand. Maybe you understand as well." It's this recurring presumption that wedges inside and rots: a client's complete, arrogant confidence that he is as emotionally significant in your life as you are in his, or that he can treat you badly and you'll have to accept it, or that there will be no consequences if he robs you (of your money, your sexual agency, your sense of safety). All of it stems from a failure to recognize the terms of the relationship and, unforgivably, the escort's right to her own realness, her personhood—to persist in her existence once she leaves his hotel room. I remember this man for his keloids, for his gapped teeth and the physical revulsion that surged inside me when I touched him, and for his deranged, yearslong campaign of abuse. On the rare occasion when I think of him, I google his name, hoping to see proof that he's dead.

My revenge-seeking friend daydreamed about telling her most despised clients exactly what she thought of them. She didn't merely want her freedom or the money she was owed; she wanted to make them suffer. But when I truly disliked someone, I just wanted to not have to talk to or think about him ever again. Removing myself from his life without explanation was the most definitive way to assert my autonomy while revealing the limits of his own.

I REMEMBER JUST ONE man who was saturated with disregard for me in the way anti–sex work activists imagine all clients are, and his attitude was so foreign that trying to recall it now feels like summoning an obscure academic fact as opposed to a personal experience. We spent three bleak, hotel-bound days together right before Thanksgiving, and that time left only a vague impression of unpleasantness. I can't remember sleeping on that trip, though I must have. I can't remember the bed, can't remember if he snored. Can't remember much of his body. Can't remember how it felt to be in my own. It couldn't have been that terrible. There was no trauma, no moment I've been forced to relive in my mind. But I remember how his misanthropy crawled down my throat like an idle, well-fed spider. And I remember the view. From the windows, Chicago was a dystopian emptiness, the streets below swirling with snow and an occasional pedestrian staggering against the wind.

He liked to keep the TV on. The TV, much more than my company, was his vacation. And it wasn't a smoking room—no rooms are smoking rooms—but he smoked constantly. As I sat next to him, pretending to watch a VH1 documentary about a minor band from the '90s, he told me to suck him off. I unzipped his pants without his help and struggled them off his backside while he begrudgingly heaved up his hips from the couch. He didn't look at me or talk to me because the TV was more interesting, though he reached down and pinched my nearer tit with the force of someone gripping the fat around their own waist.

Some men would have eroticized my submission, fluffed up their sense of dominance in that moment. That was what I got a lot of when I worked on a webcam. *Yeah, you like that, don't you, you nasty slut. Gag on it. Say you love it.* But to want to degrade someone, you have to recognize they contain a quality—a soul, a sense of self, an integrity—that can be degraded. And I might as well have been a Roomba gliding over his dick. He was that fabled villain who treated other people like inanimate objects because that was how he saw them. Most clients don't want sex to be that way. Most people don't. Even if a man has a predilection toward sadism, he wants to know he's with another human being.

An escort friend of mine met this man before I did and said

he told her a story about intentionally hitting a cyclist with his car without stopping to see if he—or she?—was OK. "This sums up his respect for humans in general," she emailed me in her reference. "I almost left the date right then." And yet she didn't. "He's not a cop," she told me, "and he's good for the $." The money was my excuse for taking the booking despite her anecdote, just as it was her excuse for staying for the rest of the date, but I didn't need the money badly enough to use the word "need," and I doubt she did either. I was there because of my curiosity and my arrogance, and many escorts I've known, the expensive ones anyway, are the same. Barring a history of nonpayment, stalking, or physical abuse, we say yes because we believe we're tough and special. We want to prove that our peers don't have our unique skills—they can't seduce or civilize the way we can. We also find ways to dress up the greed; we pretend we're Robin Hood, reclaiming money from bad people to spend it among the good (ourselves, our lovers, our friends). We convince ourselves the money is better off anywhere else than with the Man—than with That Man, at least.

Hubris may be a symptom of the stigma. We develop distorted ideas about how to prove we have worth, flimsy methods of convincing ourselves we're better than the others in our position, though we love and like—and rely upon—others in our position. A year later, I tried to explain to an escort in LA what this man was like, just to warn her. He'd sought her out because I'd mentioned she was a friend. She replied with a

tolerable amount of condescension: "I'll try to soften him up."
She emailed again after eight hours in his company to tell me
she'd bailed on their multiday date. I spent more time with him
than anyone I know.

I took pride in being able to endure. I cherished my stub-
bornness as much as I coveted the money. Maybe that was my
talent, my trade secret: that I'd inherited the selfish obstinance
of my father. It was how I affirmed and sustained self-respect;
I didn't give up because I didn't have to. And I wasn't worried
because I believed in my power and control. Sometimes they
asked if I was afraid. One man tied me up and went through
my purse, but I'd left my ID at home and he couldn't tie a knot
for shit—and he, like the man from Chicago, hovered over the
DNS ("do not see") list. (The BDSM agency he'd given as his
reference said two girls had blacklisted him, but one hadn't.) No,
I wasn't afraid. I felt no alarm, only disdain for his ineptitude.

Whatever the men told themselves about who had the upper
hand, I was my only boss. And I was there to prove something
to myself, to undergo a ritual. It felt less like I was testing myself
than that I was testing the world, waiting for something to give.
It wouldn't be me.

Each day in that Chicago hotel room, I shut the bathroom
door and stared at my own eyes in the mirror. I would have had
the look I usually had in private with my reflection at work: the
suspicious and conspiratorial gaze of a woman studying her double, seeing herself when she was not quite herself—I mean, seeing

myself not quite myself. My self was in a vault; that was what made the work possible then. In a vault even I couldn't open. It didn't matter whether the date lasted three hours or three days, whether I adored him or could hardly stand him—I always left with a part of me he hadn't touched, a piece locked in a place without a key, without a door. An invincible dignity. An irreducible core. No other moments in my life made me so aware of its existence.

That was what I saw in the mirror every time: myself, and a strangeness flashing inside myself, like the scales of a fish in deep water. I was in a pact with the strangeness, which sustained me. A pact to keep going until we'd had enough, until we got what we came for: the money and what it meant.

V

Near the end of 2012, on the evening of one of our now-numerous overnights, Roger said he needed to speak with me about something of consequence. He didn't say he'd fallen in love with me. He didn't use the word "love" at all. And unlike some clients who sat me down for this sort of heart-to-heart, he didn't pledge to leave his wife or give me a chunk of money to take me off the market. But he made his meaning clear. He explained that over the year and a half that we'd known each other, he'd developed feelings that violated the nature of our relationship.

I listened as I usually did while on the clock, cloaking my immediate reaction until I could discern what the client required or expected of me in response. These emotional disclosures were a perpetual hazard, and their arrival signaled the beginning of the relationship's end. I wanted clients to be enamored with me, because I made more money and could sometimes get away with doing less when they were. But to fall so in love that they needed to seriously discuss it with me was a sign of their descent into needy mistress mode—wanting more than was on offer, resenting what they were given. The relationship cracked under the pressure of their unrequited intensity, and one or both of us would eventually find it too miserable to continue.

Roger was such a measured, sober-minded person that his declaration could have been the prelude to a breakup intended to preempt his debasement and suffering. But in the moments after his confession concluded, I realized he didn't expect me to do anything with this information besides have it. He wasn't proposing that our relationship change. He seemed a little worried that I would be offended or mad at him for his feelings and that the news would make me uncomfortable. He was giving me the chance to decline seeing him again if it did. I told him I appreciated his honesty and that I liked spending time with him. As long as he liked spending time with me, too, I said, we should keep doing it. So we did.

ROGER WAS ONE OF my best clients in both senses of the term. He hired me regularly for long dates, and he was easy to be with, obliging. I wouldn't have spent time with him for free, not platonically or sexually, but I appreciated him. I didn't want to lose him as a customer, though for our first three years together, it might not have impacted my income much if I had. In 2012, I had two hundred work dates and Roger accounted for only twelve of those. Sometimes I couldn't see him because I was already spoken for, and sometimes I turned down other clients' requests because I'd promised the day to him. I was at the height of my popularity, and every client seemed expendable.

Roger's money was interchangeable with everyone else's, but I recognized the ways in which he was special. Clients are obsessed with learning their sex workers' "real" names—it's not uncommon for them to demand that information within a few minutes of meeting, though wilier ones come up with some excuse for why they "need" it, like wanting to transfer funds a certain way. No amount incentivized me to give it up in those years. I protected my name as ferociously as I would a newborn baby, and I'd stop seeing men who fixated on it or who raised any other alarm around my anonymity. But I gave my name to Roger when he requested it so he could use his frequent-flier miles to send me business class across the Atlantic. He didn't address me that way until three years after, when I gave him permission to, if he wanted. He did.

His expression of love was handled similarly. Neither of us brought it up again—it was delicate information; we were too polite, and there was no need—but it was there, like a fleece blanket between a sheet and a comforter. We each took from it what suited us. For him, I suppose, it was the love itself, and the confidence that I liked him enough to allow it, while his devotion gave me extra assurance that I could count on his business and his impeccable manners. He didn't prompt me to tell him I felt the same. Instead, he gave every indication that he expected and desired nothing more from me than what I already provided. Because of his forbearance, a reality that ruined the relationship in most circumstances instead made ours easier.

In 2013, he asked for a print of one of the pictures on my website, a sepia-toned one in which I sat naked except for thigh highs decorated in Lichtenstein-like comic panels. My hair fell across my face, with my knees knocked and my arms crossed to hide the dirty bits, and my mouth was closed in a bemused smile, so the overall impression wasn't one of solicitation. It was more like a vintage pinup, coy but wholesome and girlish, almost innocent. He wanted to put an image of me in his office, he said, and he thought this one had enough style that it could pass as a shot of a stranger he'd liked for its artistic merits. Also, other pictures on my site showed even less of my face, if they showed it at all.

I gave it to him as a birthday present, framed, and he sent me a picture of it tucked alongside the inner wall of one of his bookshelves. Visitors wouldn't spot it unless they entered the room and stood at an odd angle. My cleavage and my single peeking eye faced photos of his kids that were displayed outward for all to see: him holding and kissing his laughing son; his daughter posed in a studio's Christmas scene; his son again, this time aged out of his blond hair, with his arms crossed, wearing a karate gi.

In 2014, Roger bought a condo in DC, where we'd first met and where I lived. We spent probably half of our time there because if he wasn't already in town for work, it was easy to pretend to his wife that he needed to be. He started to read aloud to me in bed before sleep. He picked the book, always one of P. G. Wodehouse's Jeeves novels, and kept our place with a bookmark.

He brought it with him when we traveled. He missed the bedtime rituals he'd shared with his children, I think, when they would receive his ministrations with spellbound admiration. For a time, I saw this as a chauvinistic and paternal character flaw and felt that he was infantilizing me by putting me in the place of a quietly receptive, naive-acting audience. But on reevaluation, I could see it as a type of caregiving, or playacting of the same, like tucking in and rocking a doll to sleep. I'm not a doll, I'm a woman, so there was still some cause for offense. Yet I couldn't get that angry about an instinct toward tenderness or a surfeit of loving feelings that materialize without soliciting reciprocity—or any diversion that kept him happy and let me rest.

Less than a year later, in 2015, I moved to New York, and while it didn't really impact how often we got together, I know Roger was sad. He'd wanted to feel like we sometimes lived in the same city, if not the same home. He loved to play house with me, to cook bad meals and play board games and fall asleep on the couch while watching TV. I was still using the ATM card to pay myself and we didn't discuss numbers, though from time to time he mentioned that he planned to make a deposit. There seemed no obstacle to our going on like this indefinitely.

THOUGH ROGER WAS ASSIDUOUSLY honest with me, he didn't extend the same courtesy to his wife. I wondered about her, as I wondered about most clients' spouses, with lazy yet broad curiosity. Did the wives permit their husbands' infidelity while feigning ignorance? Were they relieved to be free from the imposition of sex? At home, did the spouses speak to each other lovingly, touch each other casually? Were they physically affectionate, or was all skin-to-skin contact gone?

Bed death was the excuse offered by clients who felt obligated to explain why they were in a committed relationship and also naked with me, and to their credit it was normally presented with resignation but not accusation or enmity. "We don't have sex anymore" held both parties responsible—or neither, as if they were just adapting to a circumstantial change, like they'd sold their sailboat or their outdoor cat had gone missing. If there really had been years of little to no erotic intimacy, surely the wives could figure out how the husbands coped. Maybe the wives coped by using adultery, too.

Sometimes hysterectomies were cited, or chronic illness, or resistance to a specific, obsessive predilection. If a client had an easily indulged fetish, like foot worship, I'd encourage him to explain to his wife how important it was to him, so she'd have a proper opportunity to join in. But the strength of the shame meant that any whiff of "no" tended to linger for years, and the guy was usually so afraid of treating it with the seriousness it deserved, he'd make the request sound like a short-lived whim. If she laughed it off or made a face or asked him why they would do that with each other, he'd never mention it again. That misunderstanding impeded the creation of new intimacy and pushed them apart. Couples don't have to share everything with each other, but this, to me, was an unnecessary loss.

Then again, no matter how innocuous I thought the fetish was and no matter how effectively a husband conveyed his investment in it, the wife's refusal could be absolute. One client whose wife had cheated on him (with his friend!) developed a cuckold fantasy that she wouldn't go along with no matter how many times he asked. He didn't want her to start sleeping with someone else again; he just wanted her to pretend that she was while they fucked and to tell him how inferior he was in comparison. I remember this man for a lot of reasons, mainly because he was young and attractive and his dick was big, which made it difficult to belittle with a straight face. But that was all right, because looking at his erection and laughing fit the scene. His response to her betrayal seemed like a dream to me: he stayed with her *and* turned it into a source of pleasure. What more could this woman want?

A lot of fetishes were more fun and less torturous than the excessive genital stimulation work often entailed, so I was glad when clients asked for them, and I learned a lot about my capacity for arousal when they did. The only way to find out how you actually responded to these sorts of things was by doing them. And if it wasn't hot, it could still be fascinating. An air traffic controller asked for a role-play in which I poisoned him and then, as he lay dying on the floor, I called my lover and laughed about how we'd finally be rich with my dead husband's money. He came, from what I could tell, in his pants while fully clothed, lying on his back on the hotel room floor. He closed his eyes like I'd pulled a thorn from his side and thanked me.

It delighted me to glimpse people's shadowed spots, the hidden recesses rarely visited even by themselves. I didn't understand why any wife would want to stay out. Didn't marrying the man indicate a willingness, if not a desire, to know him completely by sharing these sorts of private proclivities? But the implication of sharing is different when it's someone you're bound to. For me, a divulgence was simply interesting or amusing, but for some wives, perhaps, it happened within a context of long-standing imbalance or failure. If they felt neglected or put upon or rejected in their own ways, those sides of their husbands may have been irritating, disconcerting, disappointing, or they may not have had the energy to care. I think I handled my privileged information with respect. But it didn't mean much to me because, usually, neither did the man.

I WONDERED ABOUT THE wives, but I wondered about the husbands, too. Some of them had plenty of sex at home. And some had gorgeous wives, young and vibrant wives, at least from what I could see in the images that came up when I googled the man's name during screening. (Unsolicited, they might show me pictures during our appointment, not only of their wives but of their kids, in-laws, pets, and homes. Because I'm nosy, I loved it.) One man said his wife was a former model; another bragged that his wife never ate carbs. Yet another showed me a picture of his wife in lingerie to illustrate her fitness. They knew how attractive their partners were and how much time their wives spent alone while they themselves were away for work (and "for work"). Yet they didn't worry about being on the other end of the cheating. I suspect their complacency came from knowing they had the money, and that their wives were unlikely to forfeit their lifestyles and incite the gossipy local scandal of a divorce. The husbands may also have assumed their wives were too busy with the kids.

The ones who were most emphatic about how much they loved their wives were usually the worst when it came to misrepresentation in other matters. They claimed they only wanted to see one prostitute regularly, but in fact they hired new women wherever they went. They'd say, "I hardly ever do this," then use me as a reference for a string of other girls in close succession. And they'd say they wanted a true emotional connection while they armored themselves with ego and disinterest. I can't say how much these men did or didn't love anyone in their lives, but the way they described themselves had little correlation with the choices they made. The dissonance highlighted that what love meant to them might not be what it meant to their spouses or to me. "Relationships are hard," I said insipidly to one of these clients as he opined about his cheating, when I couldn't think of what else he wanted to hear. "No, I don't think so," he replied.

The best men would talk about their spouses with warm nonchalance, like I was any other service professional, someone who cut their hair or a personal trainer. They'd come to terms with what they were doing and why they were doing it, so it wasn't a threatening, forbidden topic. They could just relax and speak about this important person as the conversation warranted, without defensiveness. Even from men I found awful, I don't remember any "my wife is a bitch" rants, probably because clients didn't want to spend their time with me thinking about their wives. One San Francisco regular of mine complained that his wife didn't give him enough blow jobs, but that sort of juvenile self-pity was rare—and his wife was a woman fifteen years his senior whom he married because she was extremely rich. If clients said anything about their partners that could be construed as negative, it mostly pertained to the dissolution of intimacy, and was regretful and sad.

My allegiance was forever shifting between the two, the husband and his invisible wife. Sometimes a tender, mild-mannered client who was especially talented in bed would say his wife denied him and I'd feel so bad for him and so unhappy with her, angry that she was wasting him and hurting his feelings. Throw the fish back if you're not going to eat it. More often, on my back, I'd think about how well I understood the wife, how refusal was the only conceivable stance; if I could have outsourced or refused this onerous chore, I would have. You may want to think this was a matter of personal preference, and a different woman would have been overjoyed to fuck the man in question. But I think some guys would be fobbed off on someone else until they died.

Whether or not a wife sounded likable, I knew I usually had more in common with her than with him. The clients, almost all of them, made a strong case for the impossibility of male fidelity. Any person can be cheated on at any time, but it feels like a uniquely humiliating and female position to be put in. More than that, my identification with the wife was based on my assumption that she and I both hated having sex with him or listening to him bloviate, yet we relied on him for money. And this key commonality rendered us enemies or at least rivals. I didn't see it as a strictly her vs. me struggle, and it wasn't that I wanted any wife left destitute, but her presence limited his freedom, and he couldn't hire me if he didn't have time to himself. Family trips in particular took the husbands and therefore their money away from me. I felt put out by those.

Roger clearly respected his wife a great deal—he may have used those words, as that was how he spoke, in phrases like "a great deal"—but it seemed to me that their relationship was characterized by coldness. He wasn't allowed to refer to her as his wife, for instance, because she found the word "wife" demeaning and wanted him to use "spouse" instead. He planned an elaborate and expensive birthday party for her when she hit a milestone age, but when he reached one of his own, the celebration she arranged was cursory and uninspired. Though he petitioned for it, they'd not had sex in many years, and based on what he valued in our dates, she didn't care to hear about his job or his thoughts on a myriad of other topics. It sounded as if she didn't like him at all.

Given the scant reports I had to go on, my version of her was brittle and humorless, more shrewish and emasculating than any other wife in the pantheon of projections that formed in my head. But Roger was complicit. He could have afforded a divorce, but he didn't divorce her, which meant the situation suited him to some extent. He was not a demonstrative man. He didn't cultivate an environment of warmth and play. Plus, he'd married her in the first place, and he was perceptive enough to know what he was getting at the time. His description of their premarriage relationship wasn't dissimilar from its present shape, so there was no idyllic time he hoped to return to. In the memories he shared with me, an idyllic time had never existed.

IN 2016, ROGER AND I went to a resort in Montana. Our first night there, he was worn out by the travel and time change and went straight to sleep. The second night, again, he was too tired for anything physical. During the third day, he went on a mountain biking excursion that proved too intense for him. He came to bed sore, feeling old and unhappy. On the fourth night, he drank too much—not so much that he threw up or embarrassed himself, but enough that he didn't want to be intimate. On the fifth day, about a half hour before we were supposed to meet our ride to the airport, he said to me, "We haven't made love on this trip."

A strong argument could be made that this was my fault and that my job as an escort was to initiate sex a few times, if not act constantly horny and initiate it a lot. I knew Roger wasn't lodging a complaint against me, though, because I never acted that way with him, and he'd preemptively stated he wasn't up for sex most of the evenings. But I didn't like that he was bringing it up.

"That's okay," I said. "Our schedule was so full—there were so many other things going on, and you didn't feel well."

"When do we have to meet our driver?" he asked, and my stomach sank. What followed felt worse than usual because it seemed obligatory on both our parts instead of only mine. The sex, short and incomplete as expected, gave him no peace. I knew he was thinking of his wife and their sexlessness, wondering how culpable he was in the situation he'd conceptualized as his unjust oppression. It wasn't just Montana that muted his sex drive. Even at his DC condo, we had sex only every other time we met, and because of his snoring, I slept in the guest bed. How was our relationship different from the one he had with his wife, if the sex had now seeped out of ours, too?

It took six years (dozens of dates, hundreds of hours) for Roger to tell me he only drank red wine when away from his wife, because she didn't like the smell. He sounded aggrieved when he said it; he wanted not just to drink the wine but to share it, and this was another pleasure she denied him. Yet when he had the opportunity to select a partner to this specification, he instead attached himself to me, a woman who wouldn't fulfill his modest, unspoken wish because I don't drink. As if he needed a bottle-size disappointment in a relationship to recognize it as significant.

A lot of compulsive behavior can be understood as an attempt to learn the unlearnable, to teach yourself something you're failing to learn. Whatever insight you're chasing might be categorically unknowable, or beyond your specific capacity, or maybe you trap it but almost instantly lose it, and so track it down again, committing the same mistakes while you do. The mistakes can become a component of the sequence, the superstition. The mistakes might not be distinguishable as such. Maybe, no matter how inefficient or painful, they're not mistakes at all.

Roger and I were compatible: serious, sedentary, unobtrusive, cat-loving introverts, thoughtful about how we expressed ourselves and scrupulous about honoring each other's boundaries. We enjoyed storytelling and intellectual challenges. We disliked drawing the attention of strangers. For us, being quiet and comfortable was a luxury that trumped most others. But these traits aren't rare—not among prostitutes, not among clients. And they don't automatically foster affinity or attachment. I don't think Roger chose me because I'm so exceptional, though maybe I was exceptionally suited to him. I believe I felt familiar to him in ways outside of my, or his, control.

Roger thought he wanted to augment his marriage, but instead, something in him wanted to fashion a new union along the lines of the old, this version more stylish or flashy perhaps, yet with a structure essentially the same. Such idiosyncratic preferences are obvious when they're sexual—when they're a fetish, like being spat on or "forced" to wear pantyhose, and require coordinating with another person. It's harder to see the emotional needs that satisfy themselves without our conscious involvement, quietly, over longer stretches of time.

Many men gravitate toward the security and domesticity of long-term relationships. Lots of clients will re-create their primary relationship in the field that's supposed to be their escape from the same. They orchestrate it, because when it's not there, they ache for it. They may need to feel and act as if they're relationally unencumbered. They may make a show of how horribly the collar chafes or how brazenly they yank it off, but they still want the tether of home. Carousing and woman- izing aren't the same without it. A leashed dog feels the frenzy for a squirrel just out of reach, then returns to a full bowl and a fleece bed that smells of himself. An unleashed dog follows a scent into new woods, wanders exhausted into an empty field, lies down in the friendless dark.

At the start of my career, I believed sex work would teach me something about men, and it did, but fitfully. The lessons were impermanent, just pulses of knowledge. I kept glimpsing flickers. I kept trying to catch the flash. It was like fishing with bare hands. The slipperiness of wisdom—the Sisyphean strug- gle to not just achieve revelation but to make it stay put—isn't a unique challenge but a feature of the human brain. Sometimes a savant, like a Zen monk, will train so rigorously and for so long that they're able to hold the wisdom fish and show it to the rest of us, but we can't stare at someone else's fish for our whole lives. Looking isn't the same as holding, anyway. One can examine their own pathology and still be bereft of a *why*. Even rarer is the why that lingers long enough to make a change, to eliminate the need for the behavior and spoil the enjoyment of its ephemeral satisfaction.

Perhaps we let go of comprehension on purpose. When an itch subsides, so does the ecstasy of scratching it. "Such was my heart, O God, such was my heart," St. Augustine wrote, reminiscing about his "carnal corruptions," those old delights so vivid and near. "It was foul, and I loved it."

I THOUGHT ABOUT MARRIAGE sort of abstractly, as a concept, because I was a satellite of so many others'—indirectly but sometimes directly, too. I didn't like seeing couples, but I didn't turn them down if they passed screening and sent a deposit. They'd book me together a few times or just once and then, almost without fail, the man would contact me on his own and ask that I not tell his other half. I met a few cheating wives that way, too. They'd hire me with the men they were cheating with, men who were married to someone else as well. Once, a woman hired me with her lover and then, feeling guilty, hired me with her husband, who'd never slept with another woman before and didn't want to sleep with me. He indulged his wife in her request, though, because he loved her.

But I didn't think about marriage as having any bearing on me or pertaining to my future. It seemed like holding political office or getting a scuba certification, a folly I had no interest in trying to pursue. When I was a girl, my daydreams were about animals and opulence and my friends, not a wedding or a husband. I wanted companionship and connection with a man, but marriage wasn't the form it took in my mind. Into my thirties, I answered, "I'm too young to be married!" whenever someone asked, and I meant it.

Marriage seemed to be the domain of old-fashioned, dull minds, people who embraced societal norms and wanted to lead the least challenging lives they could manage.

That was my more generous interpretation of it, anyway, since work illustrated on a regular basis that marriage was a cynical, manipulative deal maintained through liberal amounts of lies if not wholly undertaken in dishonesty. Before work, I'd had my parents, who acted as a cautionary tale about the futility of monogamy—both requesting it and expecting it. Marrying someone to seal in sexual commitment was like putting ice in a Styrofoam cooler and believing it would never melt. Or maybe it was more like putting ice in a preheated oven.

Through grade school and beyond, I liked to think my parents' divorce hadn't affected me that much because I'd been so young when it happened. I've always felt grateful to them for getting it over with quickly instead of drawing it out. Really, I only have my mom to thank for that, since my father would have stayed unfaithfully married to her for as long as she'd let him. But my earliest memories are of their terrifying, screaming fights; my younger brother crying in the middle of the night in my dad's new house; me crying in my dad's arms as he took me from the car to my mother; homesickness sloshing around inside me at school and even at home, forever threatening to spill over my surface.

I assume my parents came to mind when my friend's name-less, devirginizing brother took off my underwear, because I'd been mulling over how to avoid re-creating all that pain. *I was thinking the other day about how my parents ruined one another, how much they ruined in each other,* I wrote in my journal a few months before the unhappy event. *Replaced the good things with something ugly and sad. That's depressing. But I know I won't make that same mistake because at least I can realize that men weren't meant for monogamy.* I wanted to treat sex the way men did, not so much for sexual pleasure but for the pleasure of confirming the self, ego-boosting, and entertainment. I did not want to volunteer to be the victim.

Sexual practice with the boys felt safe because of this dimension, too. There was no implication of my wanting or expecting them to be monogamous with me, so I wouldn't be made a fool of when they hooked up with some other girl. And, really, monogamy wasn't my wish any more than marriage was because I could only conceive it as lifestyle by fiat. I wanted my crush Noah to fall in love with me, but I didn't want to have sexual ownership over him or for him to exert that degree of control over me. I just wanted us to share an intensity of attraction that would, presumably, block out interest in others. I wasn't great at framing my decisions back then in terms of my desires, but I could still clumsily act toward them, like a mole bumbling toward a light.

I KNOW FOUR ESCORTS who married and got pregnant by men who'd hired them, and at least one of them, whether she loved him or not, continued to think of her husband as a client for years after the birth of their child. So many people marry for money that this attitude is only scandalous because it is so blunt and self-aware. Two of the women seemed to settle into the more conventional habit of seeing their respective husbands as romantic partners, like boyfriends, but they continued to see the men as financial providers first and foremost. One euphemism for an escort is "provider"; that parallelism illustrates the elegance of the exchange. I can see how marriage to a client might be better than marriage to a civilian. It probably lessens the emotional risk by circumventing the insecurity and jealousy that so often plague romantic bonds, and it gives the union a clear purpose—for the sex worker, anyway. Clients can be so self-deluded. They aren't always capable of recognizing what the bargain entails on their end.

I didn't fall for any of my clients. I cared for a lot of them and sometimes became infatuated, but that was as far as it went. I've long loved daydreaming for its own sake. I knew that outside the container of the paid encounter, the emotional contents would begin to spoil. The paid date made us each into edited versions of ourselves that disintegrated once we forfeited our roles. Even the sexual chemistry wasn't immune to decay.

The best work dates didn't feel like real life. They were more vivid, more compelling, than most encounters, like a drug trip, because they concentrated energy by removing distractions. Then we each could make the other person our sole focus. The way to savor the experience wasn't by dismantling the structure in which we'd met but by spending as much time in the paid encounter as possible. Most of the men I really liked seemed to understand that. It wasn't coincidental that those same men had no interest in leaving their wives.

IN 2017, A FEW months after our Montana trip, Roger entered a period of prolonged brooding that made our last visit of the year a somber one. He told me that if his wife wasn't willing to reestablish some form of physical intimacy with him, or at least make a move in that direction, he needed to end their relationship and begin looking for a new one. The implication was that our arrangement would end then, too, because once he was without the life partner I propped up, my role would be taken on by her (improved) replacement. He said he felt like Frodo preparing to climb Mount Doom. I told him I was proud of his resolve and wanted him to do whatever was necessary for his happiness.

Our communication during the ensuing months was infrequent. "I am still trying to figure out if I think my mission is to destroy the gold ring I bear," he emailed me a few weeks after our November date. "Also, Frodo never recovered fully from the wounds he suffered on his quest and could not resume his prior life in the Shire." I didn't write back to that because I didn't know what to say. Two years before, in 2015, I'd taken down my advertisements and work website and quit seeing new clients. I saw a handful of "trusted friends" in addition to Roger, but he had accounted for at least half of my income since semiretirement. His Sturm und Drang was exasperating to me on its own, and the prospect of losing what amounted to a salary was extra irritating. I might have been more compassionate if he'd kept meeting with me in person, but unpaid and from a distance I wasn't a very sympathetic ear.

At the end of January, Roger updated me with the message that an impending trial was giving him the "excuse" to move to the DC condo. In March, he sent me a long letter titled "Report from Exile." It was a diaristic depiction of some of his progress since the day after Thanksgiving, when he initiated the big conversation with his wife.

The Issue was raised, but like a bill a committee does not want to pass, the motion was laid upon the table. The Issue is legitimate, it merits attention. The voice was passive: the Issue should be addressed; the problem should be solved. By whom and when, though, were adjourned sine die. December gives way to January and February is looming and the committee has not reconvened.

The Party of Passive Aggression points out that maybe my absence will punish Her for the hurt (all without me having to actually admit that I have been hurt). The Party of Self-Denial tells me I will have less of an appetite if I am not spending all the time looking at an empty place setting. The party of What Else Are You Gonna Do asks, "What else are you gonna do?"

But there is a dissenting voice: the Party of Is This Really a Good Idea. It does not oppose Exile, but it asks uncomfortable questions. It reminds me that passive aggression is a lousy coping strategy with a long and inglorious history of failure. It wonders how likely Self-Denial will lead to a permanent, happy solution. Isn't the Exile project really an experiment in how lonely you can make yourself? Is that really a good idea?

I announce the Exile plan, but only to You.

He ended by saying he brought up the issue again to his spouse while she drove him to the airport. He asked her if she remembered their conversation, and she said yes, to which he said, "Not much has changed." She responded, "I want to make you happy," and her wording—as opposed to "I want you to *be* happy"—gave him a modicum of encouragement.

He'd capitalized my pronouns before, but only when he was writing to me in his most literary tone after we'd spent some time apart and he had no proposed date for when we'd next meet. Dominatrixes sometimes demand it of their submissives, or the submissives do it spontaneously. It's also, of course, how some supplicants address God. Roger capitalized his wife's pronoun this time, too.

FOR ROGER, THE ULTIMATUM was a major emotional development poised to initiate one of the most significant turns of his life. But I was fairly confident that once he posed it to his wife, she wouldn't do anything, and neither would he. It had been like that for most of their marriage, so why would it be different now? People can decide to leave unsatisfying relationships after years of endurance and that decision isn't always tied to the kids going off to college, as Roger's now had, or an existential crisis–prompting brush with death or some other dramatic event. One client of mine left his wife of ten years while the kids were still in grade school because his dissatisfaction finally pushed him past the constraints of his inertia and fear. But that man didn't love his wife and he didn't agree with her parenting choices. They were only glued together by his risk aversion.

Roger's issue wasn't really the absence of sex but the fact that he'd permitted the sex to be absent for decades and now his stamina—to put it more bluntly, his virility—was in decline. The unfortunate convergence of his sixtieth birthday and Trump's election, which he described as "an anchor dragging my spirits through the muck," pushed him into depression. His marriage may have seemed to him the sole stressor under his control and therefore the only problem he could target for solution, but he would have hated the consequences of following through on his threat.

I'm sure there are plenty of women who would have married Roger if he were single, but he was too passive when it came to romance and always had been. He told me so, and I witnessed it. Given his current melancholia especially, it was impossible to imagine him being excited to go on a first date or to log in to matchmaking sites with anything other than beleaguered fatigue. I didn't think his wife would believe that he'd divorce her. I certainly didn't. But maybe if he made good on his promise, it would spark an internal revolution that would turn him into a lothario.

After six months of masochistic sequestering, Roger reached the expected decision. He would give up on sex with his wife forever, accept their marriage for what it was, and continue seeing me—an ostensible defeat or at least a surrender. But the introspection during his time alone improved his morale and generated new enthusiasm for travel complete with luxury accommodations and activities. He was especially excited about the prospect of our ten-year anniversary. He thought it would be in 2020, which would have been a year and half away if he'd been right, and he wanted us to start thinking about the best way to celebrate.

But he was wrong, and I told him so; we'd met in 2011, so 2021 was our anniversary, and I could prove it because I still had the first email he sent me. I didn't correct him on many points, but this error and his attendant giddiness nettled me too much to let it slide. I was mad that he'd spent so long dithering only to return to the status quo, and annoyed that he was being sentimental after voluntarily (and, to my mind, pointlessly) separating from me. Thanks to his hiatus, I made less in 2018 than I had in any of the previous ten years.

Roger also began to talk about retirement, though he claimed that his coworkers, family, and I ("everyone" he mentioned it to) reacted to this with tacit disapproval, which he interpreted to be financially motivated. For me it was, but probably not as he thought; I simply didn't see how we'd spend time together if he didn't have work as his excuse for getting away. Perhaps his lack of concern about that obstacle was proof that he was formulating a plan for how to manage anyway. He always had a solution to those sorts of challenges. But I wondered if his wife's lack of enthusiasm was a mirror of mine: not about the lost income, but the prospect of his spending more time at home.

VI

IV

One of the first mini vacations of Roger's new fun era was to involve us traveling to an inconveniently located Michelin three-star restaurant for dinner and spending the next day at a nearby spa. The logistics required more correspondence than usual, and in the course of our exchange, his emails began to unnerve me. At first, the errors were nothing that would give another person pause: a few typos here and there, and confusion about details that could be attributed to careless reading of my previous message or a hastily composed response on his part. But hasty and careless were not Roger's style.

He told me he'd been having blurred vision and debilitating headaches, and then the mistakes made more sense. He facetiously said that he'd "ruled out a stroke" by doing his own research online and surmised his symptoms were related to pollen. I knew that aging had become difficult for him. He was increasingly sensitive to inconvenience and indulged in bouts of overwrought self-pity after any brush with physical vulnerability: an especially cold visit to Chicago; feeling tired earlier in the evening than he used to; being outpaced by a younger man on a neighboring treadmill. He was overly cautious and easily flustered while driving, and once I'd missed my train because of his disorientation, though he lived only fifteen minutes from the station.

He saw a doctor who told him to get a brain scan, but that was all he shared with me—that, and his irritation with the recommendation. By then he had trouble keeping his balance when he walked and said I'd need to drive the car while we were together because of the ongoing issue with his sight. A terrible foreboding bubbled up in me. I no longer believed he was exaggerating. On the contrary, his lack of urgency inflamed my anxiety more than his other symptoms did. His reticence to complete the necessary diagnostics could have been denial or fear, but it seemed like something worse—his mind failing him, not his nerve. I couldn't tell what was going on, and I didn't know how to get more information. His communication was all I had.

I repeatedly tried to put off our trip. Each time, he replied that he would be fine, and with every attempt I worried I bruised his ego while coming across as maternal and nagging: two of the worst things a service professional or a girlfriend can be. One of my primary duties was to figure out a way for him to never hear "no," not because he was a tyrant or I was his slave, but because my job was to make his life better. He made it easy because I rarely needed to say no to him. I had to say "I can't" when he wanted to see me on a day when I wasn't free, but he didn't put me in positions where I had to refuse him. He asked for so little, and what he proposed was often tedious but never unreasonable given the shape of our arrangement.

I insisted he at least get the scan before we met, and he assured me he would "today or tomorrow," though the timing of it seemed impossible since it was Saturday when he replied. But he was a wealthy and competent man. Maybe he could schedule an appointment in the morning before we were to meet. Maybe a friend who happened to be a neurologist was getting him into the office on the weekend. I set aside my instincts and better judgment and on Monday traveled by train to meet him.

I texted him as I was pulling into the station, and he told me he wasn't there. He was at home, in another state. He thought it was Saturday, and he'd thought it was Saturday the day before, too, which was why he'd missed his Sunday flight, though he also seemed to think that flight wasn't until the coming weekend anyway. None of it made sense. Reading what he wrote about dates was like watching someone try to build a card tower without letting the edges touch.

"My Bad" was the title of the email he sent me that evening as I rode back to New York. It was a phrase I'd never heard him use before. He electronically deposited $1,000 into his debit account as an apology, which covered the train tickets and paid me about $500 for my day of lost time. With a normal client, I'd have collected a deposit for half of our date's full cost. It would have been many times as much, and not refundable in the event of a same-day cancellation.

I was furious, and I told him I was insulted, but I also said honestly that it didn't matter right then because all that was important was him getting care. He apologized again and said he wanted to see me in New York on the coming weekend, which made me even angrier. I told him I wasn't going to make plans to see him until he got a brain scan. Embarrassed by the missed date and (at last) shaken by his own confusion, he did.

He was right that he hadn't had a stroke. He had a brain tumor.

AFTER THREE NIGHTS IN the hospital and a battery of tests, Roger was told that he needed surgery to have the mass removed and biopsied. Radiation and chemotherapy might follow. Not all tumors are cancerous, and I told myself Roger's wasn't. I looked up statistics online and read that two-thirds of brain tumors are benign.

Despite this wishful thinking, resentment constituted much of my reaction to the news. Roger's progressively incoherent emails and the assertive, bitchy-feeling replies they warranted from me highlighted how siloed our lives were. I knew him well—maybe I knew more of him than his kids or his wife, or at least I knew him differently, because the version of him I knew was obscured from them and from everyone else. But I didn't have his health history. I had his ATM card, but I didn't have his home address. I couldn't have arranged a doctor's appointment for him no matter how badly he needed one. I couldn't even visit him in the hospital. We'd played prominent roles in each other's lives for almost a decade, but I couldn't talk to anyone in his family. No one would recognize that I meant something to him excepting, maybe, the doorman at his condo building in DC.

My helplessness and exclusion coalesced into a sense of being treated unfairly, being owed, even though Roger had already made a second electronic deposit much larger than what he'd originally sent—that wasn't the point anymore. I was experiencing a new urge to participate openly in his life because circumstances necessitated it now, and with that desire came the denial of its fulfillment. I didn't want to replace his wife or play stepmom to his grown kids or take up residence as someone romantically involved with him, a smug harpy surveying visitors as she sat by his bedside and possessively stroked his hand. I just wanted the obstacles gone because they were too difficult to maneuver around. I wanted him to give me a big chunk of money and access to his miles so I could fly down and check on him, even help him with his recovery, and not stress about rent or the cost of traveling back and forth while I did it. It felt wrong that I wasn't there. He could have fixed this if he wanted to. He didn't want to. But he still wanted me. This was what the money was for and had always been for. To compensate me for self-effacement, to help me tolerate slights and frustrations that had no solutions. And to prevent me from asking for more than what was given, because I was given a lot.

Roger's deposits made up the bulk of my income by this time, so to some extent I felt like I was facing unemployment, but I wasn't dependent on him in absolute terms. I had savings, family members who could loan or give me money, small sums from freelance writing. I could start advertising and meeting new clients again if I needed to. There were safety nets. But Roger was an all-purpose protector to me: a reassuring and trusted presence who, in an emergency, I could call on for financial support or legal guidance. It would have pleased him immensely to know I thought of him that way, but he thought of me as too strong and independent to have any sort of need for anyone.

It was easier to obsess over concrete factors, like money, than to confront my existential and actual helplessness. I thought a lot about other mistresses during those days, the ones in positions more precarious than mine because they were in love with their married men or completely relied upon them financially. When you're the other woman, there's no dignified way to announce yourself. You blast into his larger life like a bomb, or you don't enter at all. What radical loneliness those women must feel in these situations. So much loss, including the horrible finality of being closed out of his life and public record of the same.

I wasn't thinking of doing anything drastic like intentionally violating our pact of secrecy, but that didn't mean something dramatic wouldn't happen. There was so much I didn't know and could only learn by waiting: whether the surgery would work and he'd want to return to our status quo, or if the surgery would work and he'd want to stop seeing me to devote himself to his family; if the surgery would work and he'd want to leave his wife to devote himself to me; if the surgery wouldn't work and how I'd find out if it didn't. He thought that I steered our relationship, but I always followed his lead.

ROGER EMAILED ME CONSTANTLY throughout his initial hospital stay and immediately after—whether more for his sake or mine, I can't say. Our thoughts were much the same. What place would I have in his life now, if any? His body might not be capable of travel, and he might never again be unchaperoned even if it was. I could travel to him, but if doctors forbade him from being alone, then it wouldn't matter. He said he wanted to get to DC to see me, for "closure" before the surgery, which I doubted was possible, but I was prepared to make a last-minute trip if he managed it.

He mulled over the other practical aspect of our arrangement, too. "After my surgery, I may not have exclusive access to my finances," he wrote to me. "And in the worst-case scenario, my accounts transfer automatically to [my spouse]. I pulled out my will the other day and it is ironclad as far as what happens and there is not an opportunity to make changes at this point." I hadn't asked. He took all this upon himself because he wanted to give me "something that represents the strength of my regard."

This project would be beyond the scope of the ATM. He suggested he might be able to transfer stocks to me.

Roger told me on many occasions that he was glad to pay me, though he didn't use that verb. I don't think he begrudged a single dollar he spent on me. He knew money was the best way he, as a married man, could express how strongly he felt short of blowing up his life. "I want my gratitude to be tangible," he once said. "When you are walking down the street and you see something extravagant in the window, you should ask yourself, 'Would Roger want me to have this?' The answer is yes." But he wasn't especially cash-generous to any individual, aside from the grand tips occasionally given out to cabdrivers, servers, and one of our guides in Montana. He saw me as someone too principled and intellectual to be moved by financial largesse—he seemed to think this of everyone he loved, including his spouse and children—and he preferred to give away his money to institutions, especially schools. He didn't check my website for changes to my rates nor keep track of the time we spent together because he'd reduced the whole of his responsibility to simply reupping the ATM account. Our arrangement was built on a bedrock of tactful obfuscation, and it benefited me because of how it benefited him.

When I asked him for a raise, as I did a few times over the course of knowing him, he acquiesced without negotiation or pushback, though it required a single discussion to bring our expectations into alignment. I recognized that our situation offered perks most bookings didn't, but I wasn't willing to lose money by turning down other clients in order to be with him, or to resent him for paying me less than others. "I am enormously grateful that you felt ok expressing what is an awkward topic and am flattered that you trusted me enough to do it," he wrote one year in response to my mention that the account balance wasn't being properly maintained. "The biggest problem in my life arises from not addressing difficult subjects and one of the things I am most thankful for in our relation-ship is the ability to share just about anything with you." That "biggest problem," the sexlessness in his marriage that had occasioned our meeting, was why he wanted the money in the background. It reminded him not of a failure between us but a failure between him and his wife.

I didn't expect Roger to put me in his will when he was sick or when he was well, and we certainly never talked about it until he raised the topic. I assumed he wouldn't want that because I assumed my inclusion couldn't be kept a secret, though I don't know much about how wills work. There's a type of sex worker who sees being named in a client's will as the ultimate coup, proof of being the best in the game, but I wasn't hustler-brained enough for oblique, long-term schemes or even to request that clients buy me certain things or pay certain bills. I was too literal-minded, I suppose, too conservative. Inclusion in a client's will struck me as vulgar, though I wouldn't have talked anyone out of writing me into one if they were determined to do so. I just wanted to be compensated for my time and for clients to book me a lot, and I was pretty good at making that happen. The direct exchange felt fair, an honest sale.

I didn't see Roger before the surgery, but his immediate recovery went well enough that he managed a solo trip to his DC condo about a month later, and I spent the night with him there. By this time, they'd determined that he had brain cancer and it was not curable. "If I could, I'd leave you four million dollars," he told me in bed. "Five hundred thousand dollars for every year we've had together." I stayed quiet. I thought it was an uncharacteristically crass thing to say since he'd made it clear he wouldn't be able to bequeath me with so much as $5 after he was gone. To promise someone money without giving it to them is to demean both parties. But I know he meant— or thought he meant—what he said, and that he said it to indicate how much our relationship had been worth to him, though I had no idea what percentage of his wealth that number represented. Given the nature of us, this might sound silly, but it was weird of him to put a single, solid sum on it, not flattering as he may have thought. He was, unfortunately, right about my relationship with money; I could be avaricious, but I wasn't impressed by people having a lot of it nor giving it to me. If he'd left me with $4 million, it would have changed my life, but it wouldn't have changed my opinion of him or how much I believed he cared about me.

Roger did not leave me millions, or even a million. But he

did write me large checks, including one that was flagged by a banker, who sent the image of it to both Roger and his wife.

FOR THE MOST PART, Roger refrained from discussing his wife in his emails to me, but during his first hospital stay and in the days leading up to it, her absence in his updates was even more egregious. Pre-diagnosis, she was out of the country with his daughter, which was why we'd planned our ill-fated getaway when we did. But Roger had his symptoms for some time before they left. Did he not tell his family about the headaches and bad vision, or did he mention them but downplay their severity? Did he keep from his wife the news that he'd been told to get a brain scan? Roger's son, at least, knew about the initial doctor's visit because he'd had to drive Roger to the appointment. Was it not discussed with the rest of the family then, before he ended up in the hospital?

Inexplicably, Roger's wife and daughter didn't arrive home until the day of his discharge, after he'd spent seventy-two hours in the hospital with his son by his side. Were they unable to change flights? Were they assured it wasn't an emergency? (I guess technically it wasn't; it was a slower-moving tragedy.) The mystery confirmed that there was no one positioned to protect his best interests at a crucial moment and strengthened my sense of estrangement between Roger and his wife.

In retrospect, it was laughable for me to entertain the possibility that he would want to leave her for me after the diagnosis, since that was when he needed the stability and support of his family more than ever. But he'd just threatened to leave her when he thought he had decades of life left. I thought the shortening of the timeline might make seizing the day imperative, but it must have had the opposite effect; *because* he had less time left, there was no point in change. Maybe he was relieved that he'd not followed through with his ultimatum. Maybe he imagined what it would be like if he'd been separated from his wife when he discovered the tumor—living alone in a furnished local rental, buried in divorce paperwork, his children angry and confused, me dismissed from my post. I'm sure that vision would be almost too bleak to contemplate.

"I am increasingly concerned our relationship will be discovered," he wrote to me a few months after his surgery, when I suggested I come to town to visit.

The harm from discovery is even worse, given how much of her life [my spouse] is now devoting to my care. I could rationalize the injury to her feelings by comparing them to my feelings arising from our lack of intimacy. But that is really beside the point now, I think. No one could show more love and devotion than [she] is showing me these days and I want to treasure it. For you to visit right now would mean I would have to come up with multiple lies, tell them convincingly, and not get crossed up. The thought of attempting that is quite scary.

I realize this sounds like I am picking [her] over you, which I would never want to do. I am sure you would take equally good care of me but I could never ask that of you.

As his acuity declined, he became less concerned about the sophistication of his subterfuge. When the banker emailed him and his wife about the sloppily written check, for instance, Roger did not seem worried. He told his wife I was an editor he'd hired to help him with the law book he was hoping to write and didn't mention it to me again.

I remained as intrigued by Roger's wife as I ever was. I wondered if part of her was relieved to know she'd be spared Roger's entreaties about sex for the rest of her life, and that he wouldn't be able to make or deliver on any further intimations of divorce. Is it possible she thought he would die having been celibate for decades and that she might feel no regret about having refused him for so long? Did she try to absolve herself by initiating something on one of his better days? I doubt it. I'm sure Roger would have told me if she had. Instead, he mentioned that watching the movie *Wonder Woman* reminded him of me and stirred him to "physical sensations I haven't come close to since my surgery." He wrote that ten months after the procedure had taken place.

I sound monstrous, maybe. But people feel everything. It's not improbable that Roger's spouse thought selfish or cruel things and then felt guilty, or thought them and didn't. Roger's initial rosy response to her dutiful caregiving wavered considerably in the ensuing months. He told me he regretted turning over so much authority to her, and they got into at least one nasty fight about her failure to consult him when she scheduled appointments and communicated with doctors. He admitted, though, that he was depressed and probably in denial, and that he'd essentially surrendered all decision-making to (or thrust it upon) her. "I have been looking for a chance to slip the leash," he griped in one email. But the leash was on for his own good.

I'd like to say that I didn't want Roger to leave his wife, but I don't think that's entirely true. I'm a relatively impatient person, and I can be short-tempered. I hated the new limits imposed by his illness. His marriage was an inconvenience, and one he explicitly framed as a financial obstacle for me, so I resented it. But I wasn't in love with Roger, and I didn't want to marry him, so I didn't want him to leave his wife *for me.* I wanted for him to be the man he seemed to want to be: decisive and confident, unafraid of other's opinions and willing to prioritize what mattered most to him. But maybe that was exactly what he did by staying with her.

Roger was not like any other client for me; he and I used a different set of rules. But I maintained some tenets with him that I brought to all my working relationships and plenty of unpaid ones, too. I erred on the side of caution in what I said and did. I didn't pry. I didn't impose. I tried not to be a negative influence; I tried not to be manipulative. Often that meant keeping compliments and good feelings to myself, because what could be more manipulative than encouraging words from a woman you're infatuated with? Acting under those restraints for so long reinforced my emotional barriers. I pushed away many thoughts and feelings. Limit expectations; don't get too involved.

I'm still learning how it feels as those walls break down from disuse. I'm still seeing what floods in when they fall away.

AFTER HIS DIAGNOSIS, ROGER and I saw each other five more times. First, in DC, for that final overnight, then twice in his city for an afternoon. In December, we met in DC again. He was still driving, maddeningly, and insisted on picking me up from the train station. He arrived ninety minutes before I was scheduled to get in and wandered among the unhoused people while he waited. I couldn't believe his wife, who was in town with him, was fooled by his claim that he wanted time with colleagues. He drove slowly and made errors of perception, like going the wrong way down a one-way street, not responding to the traffic lights, and ignoring no-turn signs, but he seemed to think he was driving normally and indeed, many people do drive that way. He'd booked me a room at a new hotel across from his condo and stayed with me there for about three hours before he left to get back to his spouse. Two months later, I visited his city to see him for lunch. That was the last time we were together.

"My biggest fear about the future with you is that I will descend into some kind of dementia that will frustrate you and make you sad," he wrote me after the upsetting, truncated DC evening date. "Will certainly embarrass me. But mentally I think I'm still pretty together." There were mistakes in his message that I've omitted, but they weren't major; he really was pretty together. Dates, the actual day of the month and week, remained a struggle, and he said things about timing that made no sense, but he managed to plan and execute five clandestine visits for us, which was an impressive feat. He said he didn't want to be with me when he was "some invalid needing constant care and attention," and he wasn't.

Yet he was not as he had been. Once, he couldn't get out of the car, and I had to help him by trying to physically move his legs and then torso. It was challenging, and he gave a short, gruff shout of pain when I applied pressure to his leg. Once, we sat in the car for ten minutes because he either wasn't sure how to start the engine or didn't realize he was expected to. I should have stopped him from driving, but I didn't know how. It seemed his wife didn't either. It frightened me to be in the car with him; I felt held hostage by his incapacity. I didn't want to be there, so I acted as if I wasn't. I was stiff and vacant as a corpse, and not pretending otherwise because it seemed he either didn't register my withdrawal or didn't care. "Our recent visits—while quiet and low-key—were perfect for me," he wrote in between two of them. "You are a most wonderful, sensitive companion and have been a great comfort."

These meetings largely smear together into a single joyless blur. When I think of them, I see us sitting far apart in a gray room, not talking. Aside from the overnight, I don't think he took off his clothes, and I didn't take off mine. Sometimes he didn't lie down at all because it was too painful to be prone or too difficult to get up once he was. Sometimes the light hurt his eyes, so we sat in the dark. There were many dead silences, not companionable quiets but long moments in which it seemed the entire world was on pause due to technical failure.

I don't have one good memory of our last year together because the circumstances were too punishing and the version of him I saw was a diminished one, though not grotesque, not even with his head wound, nor unrecognizable. I know many people in decline worry that a lesser version of themselves will supplant memories of the superior. But I'd rather we saw each other as we did than that we didn't see each other at all. Nothing stops me from remembering who he was before. On the contrary, the fact of those five meetings proved to me that he was who I knew him to be—and I'm glad for it.

"I feel no option but to try to maintain our connection,"

he wrote. "I reread your nice words and I have you in mind all the time."

I SUGGESTED TO ROGER that he tell his brother about me, about us, because his brother was coming into town to visit while Roger's wife would be away. Enlisting his brother as our ally could have helped us arrange a lot of time together, at least doubling the length of the afternoons we'd contented ourselves with so far—and any visit could be our last. I also thought it might be a relief for Roger to finally have someone to talk to about me because he'd lamented that inability for years. I thought his brother might also be able to help us keep in touch near the end. His brother had been in an affair that broke his first marriage, and even if he weren't able to relate, surely he wouldn't deny his dying sibling this request.

I explained this to Roger when he asked why I would propose such a thing. He was quiet for a beat. Then he told me that his many siblings had all been in marriages that failed. Only he had married just once and stayed married. As far as his Irish Catholic family was concerned, he was a paragon of marital virtue, and that was a source of great satisfaction for him. He wanted his family, his coworkers, and everyone who knew him to continue believing he was a faithful partner in a sterling union.

I saw an aspect of him then that I hadn't before: his satisfaction at having gotten away with the biggest deception of his life. "I'm so looking forward to seeing you that it's hard to bear," he wrote of the few hours we'd steal under his brother's ignorance. "It's the one light in my dark universe." But it wasn't really the only light. He would die proud of having hidden me. I didn't know that about him before he got sick. I don't know if he'd known that about himself.

MY LAST VISIT WITH Roger took place on February 27, 2020. The next day, over email, he said his wife noticed some evidence of the latest check he'd written me and he "fumbled through the story" to explain. He asked me to wait a few days to deposit it, but I'd grown so paranoid about interference that I'd already fed it into an ATM a few hours before. "No worries," he replied when I apologized. That weekend, I sent him a picture of my cat and asked if there were any further issues with the check. He said no. He told me during our first visit after his surgery that he was afraid of his wife being taken in by a con man after his death, because of all the money he'd leave behind, so he evidently believed she was gullible. My notion of her, based solely on her professional accomplishments, was far shrewder.

His communication over the next month was coherent and upbeat. Occasionally, COVID was mentioned. I expected it to be a major concern given his compromised state and incessant visits to the hospital, but it didn't seem to impact him, so I rarely brought it up. We spoke throughout the week, short emails with medical updates, and jokes when he could manage them. Our correspondence over the years had been sporadic—it wasn't rare to go a full month without contact. That changed immediately after his diagnosis, when we spoke almost every day, then fluctuated with his stamina during treatment. In April, he wrote me five times, though none were about our nine-year anniversary. In May, he wrote twice.

At the start of June, Roger sent two emails on the same day. One was about his cat who liked to sleep on his chest. The other was a response to my suggestion that we might not see each other again "this year." I didn't want to be morbid, but I wanted to raise the possibility of saying whatever we might want to say before the option for saying it was gone. "My mobility issues are insurmountable," he said, waving away my suggestion that the coronavirus was the main consideration. "I can barely walk by myself with a walker." The email seemed to cut off before he finished. I sent him a link to a BBC article about the Jeeves books. I said I was thinking of him: "I miss seeing you and talking to you, and wish we had an opportunity to be together."

At the end of June, he wrote to me again: "We haven't corresponded for days and I'm sorry about that. There really isn't anything new to report." He said the chemo left him tired and immobile. He said he wanted to be an organ donor but wasn't sure how much they'd be able to salvage. After that, there was no more.

I searched online for the inevitable. Not obsessively, but occasionally. Every now and then. For months nothing turned up and I started to wonder if there might be no public announcement. I should have set up a Google Alert for his name; I don't know why I didn't think to do that. Maybe I didn't want to learn that way.

When I searched on a whim in the late fall, his obituary surfaced. He had passed six weeks after his last message. They'd picked a nice picture, one I'd seen before: his headshot from work. He was smiling. But the accompanying words, about his career trajectory and some of his hobbies, didn't feel like they had much to do with him. The style was dry, too formal. He would have written a livelier version. I skimmed the words and closed the tab. There was no acknowledgment of the family cats, though they gave him so much solace, especially in the final year. I don't know why they weren't named among his survivors, why they weren't mentioned at all.

I don't think Roger wronged me once. I have no grudges, and I don't think anything about our arrangement was unfair. In fact, it was one of the most honest and equitable and respectful relationships I've had. But Roger took away one of the biggest decisions anyone has ever taken from me when he kept me from his death.

That was his right. Even if he hadn't been paying me, or if he hadn't been married, that would have been his right. I know he did the best he could, and that it was better than most people's best would be. But we didn't get to say goodbye. It's a wound that will last forever.

On the night before his first surgery, Roger sent me an email explaining the next day's timing and letting me know when he thought he'd be awake and able to update me. He invited me to reach out to his office assistant if I hadn't heard anything by that time and wanted to find out how it'd gone. He'd prepped her to send updates to anyone who asked without the petitioner needing to identify who they were to him.

"As soon as I can contact you I will," he promised.

As I write this, I am filled with optimism that life will resume as it had before this, and I hope you will keep your spot in that life. But if that doesn't happen, you know how lucky I feel to have spent time with you. Any person in your life should dedicate themselves to being worthy of the attention you give them; I know just what a precious and valuable commodity your attention is. I wish I had more opportunity to become worthy.

If I have to distill my current sentiments down to a single sentence, the best I can do is this: no one on the planet admires or respects you more than I do. But I hope to say that and more to you in person in time.

Your Friend,

ROGER WAS SUPPORTIVE BUT unhappy when I moved to New York. He'd bought his DC condo in large part because it would be his excuse to visit the city when work didn't demand it, and when he came for a trial, we'd be more comfortable there than in a hotel. (In one of the messages before his first surgery, he told me "no one else should ever have or use the white robe" he kept for me there. This was some of what he thought about in the hospital.) Now that I'm back in DC, my weekly routine entails walking by his condo, and I look up at the balcony when I pass. I don't know what I expect to see, but it would feel wrong not to do it. For years, there was no change to the outdoor furniture. Recently, I saw it had been taken away.

Because I was so cut off from the rest of his life, because there wasn't a funeral due to COVID, because I found out about his death by googling his name months afterward, I have a hard time believing Roger is dead. I know it intellectually, but I don't experience it on a level other than the theoretical. The knowledge becomes real in moments and then leaves me again. I wouldn't be surprised if I woke up to a new email from him in my inbox. I wouldn't be surprised if I saw him on the street one day. Well, I might be a little surprised, because it's startling to see anyone you know in a place you don't expect them to be. But I'd recognize him with a certain "of course" quality. *Yes, that's him. There he is. I'd know him anywhere.* He'd be in his schlubby blue jeans and black sneakers. I'd smile and laugh and walk to him, and he'd be happy to see me, smiling, too, but we wouldn't hug on the street because we were always careful about that. Or maybe we would, just this one time. "Hi!" he would say in that slightly gravelly voice—I can hear it. I guess it's normal to feel this way even when you go to a funeral, because the world becomes wrong when some people leave it. Seeing him again would set something right, level the picture frame.

Roger's daughter's Instagram account is locked, but his son's isn't, and though he doesn't post much, I check it about once a month, sometimes as often as once a week. Roger's son is left-leaning, extroverted, expressive, dorky in the same manner Roger was dorky and in his own distinct ways, too. I've thought a lot about him having to drive to his parents' house in the middle of the night to lift Roger when he fell. It happened with some frequency as Roger's health declined, even after he had a walker. He was too heavy for his wife to manage alone. I get stuck on the notion of what that does to a young man, how it's so mundane in a way, so predictable, a cliché rite of adult passage and yet unbearably awful; how it must change the son forever, how it might scar over some places inside him and scrape others so raw that they'd never heal and there's nothing to be done about it. There's nothing to do with this sympathy I have for a man who would probably hate me if he had any idea I existed. Though Roger wouldn't hate me, I don't think, if he were in his son's position. And Roger's son seems so much like Roger.

For more than a year after Roger's death, I didn't cry about it. That worried me. Was I really such an ungrateful, Machiavellian gold digger that I wouldn't be moved by a person's passing? I didn't cry about him while he was sick either, or rather when I did, it was in frustrated, angry bursts, tears coming like a sneeze, squalls that dissipated as abruptly as they descended. I didn't wallow. But eventually, I did start crying properly. It didn't make me feel like a better person. It didn't change what had happened. I had a dream that one of us told the other, "I held you all the time," but I can't remember which of us said it.

I used to imagine a scenario in which Roger's spouse confronted me to try to get back the money he'd given me after his diagnosis. I prepared myself for accusations that I had taken advantage of his compromised state. She had my legal name because of the checks, and maybe she'd seen him emailing me, or he spoke my name as he deteriorated. I wouldn't be hard to find. No one is hard to find anymore. This possibility concerned me, yet part of me wanted it to happen. I had proof that I mattered to him when his mind was whole. I wanted to show it to someone close to him so they would know that I was included in the grief and in his life.

Roger didn't know everything about me, but he saw me. I kept a lot of myself to myself, but he was perceptive, and we spent so much time together. And I didn't lie to him or mislead him, which is a credit to him, that he didn't make me feel like I needed to. You can love someone very much without complete knowledge of them, and you usually have to, because we are enigmas even to ourselves. "While I entertained fantasies about being with you," he wrote to me once, "I could never make them work. I was never the right man for you in the long run." He wanted me to be with the right man because he wanted me to be happy.

Roger—but I am calling you by your real name now, in my head. Do you mind the name I've given you here?—I'm sorry I handled your illness badly. I know I handled it badly, but I hope you didn't feel that way; I hope I hid it from you. I tried to. If I didn't manage it, I'm sure you forgave me. But I hope you didn't have to.

You wrote to me once, when you believed you might not write to me again, about the day we spent together in Central Park, the day when you knew you'd fallen in love with me, and how you thought for years about saying the word "love" to me but "nothing good would have come of it." That's okay. You didn't say you loved me, so I didn't say I was grateful to you for loving me. And yet we told each other that. We did tell each other, many times. And good came from it.

"I can only wish that you think of me in the future with a fraction of the warmth and affection in which I will hold you," you wrote. "The loss of something precious should hurt, and to feign indifference would be an insult." Everyone takes valuable people in their life for granted, don't they, but I don't think you took me for granted, not once. That's why, at the end, you were at peace. But was it the end? Has it ended? Is it over?

Roger, I know you're gone, but I'm not sure you're really gone.

Roger, if you're still here.

If you're still here, please. Tell me.

VII

In 2014, I matched with a man named Sam on Tinder. We met at a bar in Manhattan a few blocks from my hotel in the evening after I finished with a client. He was tall and warm, with a ready smile, and we laughed side by side with our legs touching. In my room that night we had sex many times; we barely stopped. He knew I was from out of town and not looking to date or for anything regular. But when I came back to New York for work, I saw him. I came back for work again, and I saw him. I fell in love with him. I moved to the city and asked him to live with me. He did.

I know every love is incredible in the truest sense of the word, meaning so extraordinary that it exists beyond the horizon of belief—though love is also incontrovertible, the direct experience of belief itself. I'd been carried away and consumed by romantic obsession before, but I'd never loved like this. It was a state change, a metamorphosis. With him, there was everything at once: the friendship, the attraction, the passion, the fascination, the intimacy, the trust. Each element that I thought could only dance with and orbit the others was pulled into the same center and joined with so much force that they exploded, and the explosion was inside me, perpetual and permanent. I became loving, the way spark becomes flame and then stays aflame, replenishing itself with its endurance. Finding him felt like an inevitability and also a miracle. Maybe miracles are always fated.

Early into our knowing each other (too early: any self-help book would forbid it, advice columnists would call it the reddest of flags) I cried when we said goodbye. He gave me hugs like Sean had in our teenage years, with his knees bent so our chests could press, and I clung to him with my arms around his neck, hiding my face in his shoulder, nothing but need. I ached all the time. The emotions wouldn't abate, and I didn't want them to. I wanted them to burn in me forever.

I still cry when we part for days because it still hurts to be away from him. I want the maximum level of being with him. My beloved. My husband.

ANY EXPLANATION OF MY decision to marry might sound provincial and patriarchal. Perhaps my heart, desperate for superlative expression, reached down into its own depths and in lieu of inventing something new and iconoclastic, seized upon the most banal tradition. But we didn't marry because of religious alignment or pressure from our families, not because I wanted a ring—we don't wear rings—or kids or a wedding. (We don't and didn't have either.) I felt already pledged to him, and marriage seemed the starkest way to illustrate it because of what marriage (had) represented to me before him, which was nothing. I wanted to demonstrate—to myself and to him—that he was the only one I would do this for or want this with because he was the only one who could fill it with meaning. Our marriage matters to me not because I care about marriage but because I care about Sam.

Married couples like to say getting married changes everything, but I haven't found that to be true. Instead, being married reminds me of how it felt to be disabused of inherited ideas about intercourse, to finally understand that it wasn't an inherently important or enviable encounter and the bar of entry was so low that all sorts of people did it with people they didn't even like.

I admit marriage has settled me down, just a bit, like a weighted blanket. My normal instinct with romantic relationships was to think of them as so loosely knit that I could slip out at any time, and that created pressure to continually assess if it was in fact the right time to leave. That resulted in a lot of counterproductive scrutiny and occasional outright paranoia. I didn't quite recognize this tendency until I was with Sam. His parents have been married for his whole life, and they love and cooperate with each other. His model of partnering was people who have disagreements and fight sometimes yet stay together and continue to laugh with and rely on each other.

But before we were married, his reactions influenced mine, and I got better at recognizing that my willingness to quit sometimes slid into an eagerness to do so as preemptive defense. I don't object to divorce the way some people seem to, the ones determined to weather their misery-inducing marriages because of pride or conventionality or avarice. It's not like we'd be broken up if marriage weren't tying me down—we're together because we want to be together—but the marriage is a reminder. It keeps me from overreacting or lets me overreact for less time and without really meaning it.

"Marriage changes everything," at least as I've heard it, hints at an ominous quality, like marriage is a potion you wouldn't have swallowed if you'd known the effects. In that context, "commitment" becomes a word synonymous with suffering and sacrifice, a trial you withstand through sheer fortitude. Sam and I have been together long enough now that even if we weren't married, according to heterosexual norms, our relationship is supposed to be boring at best, onerous and embittering at worst, and definitely not joyful. Not rejuvenating or enlivening. "Is this allowed?" Sam jokes about how attracted he is to me. I think something similar when I moon over him, when I'm sitting across from him and our eye contact lasts longer than usual and my insides give a twirl. I'd been made to think this stage passes quickly and is lost forever, but the first feelings I had for him aren't gone. It's more like they regenerate and sprout from a mature base, the way a hearty plant buds new leaves. Once, when the plant was brand-new, the fresh growth was the whole of what was there. Now the fresh is still there, but with older growth, too.

When Sam calls me his wife to my face or around our friends, as in "Can I please sit next to my *wife* now?" I get a giddy thrill, like he's tickling me or whispering something naughty. When I overhear him talking to strangers or acquaintances, I feel like we're lying or pulling off some kind of prank. (He says into the phone, "I won't be home then, but my wife will," and part of me snickers: *Don't they know we're too young to be married?*) The word always feels loving, like an affirmation. It reminds me that he chose to call me that because he chose to make me that to him, and he chose to be that to me. I'm still getting used to our being such in the realm of public categories. It might take a long time, because when I look at him, it's even harder to conjure the possessive. I don't feel like I own him, but I know we are promised to each other, and that the promise is private, ultimately, regardless of how it glimmers into view for the rest of the world. *This is my husband's shirt*, I'll tell myself sometimes when I'm taking clothes out of the dryer, pressing the fact into my brain.

SEVEN OR EIGHT YEARS ago, when Sam and I were fairly new, I read a memoir by a writer whose husband left her for another woman. It terrified me because the author said she loved her husband dearly and that they'd had wonderful sex together throughout their marriage. Sex was one of the things they did best together; it was never lacking or underwhelming. In the book, she begs him not to leave her, and every time she convinces him to sleep with her, their sex is as intense and fulfilling as she's always known it to be. He leaves anyway. I found the book so disturbing that I instantly gave it away and wiped the title from my mind. Her anguish and abjection were so effectively conveyed that they still unnerve me. She experienced total loss: of a domestic partner, best friend, intellectual peer, confidant, live-in co-parent, and the most intoxicating lover she'd ever had.

Rationally, I know that sleeping with someone—anyone, including your spouse—doesn't keep them from sleeping with other people. But for years I thought having sex with your partner was at least a semi-reliable prophylactic against betrayal and breakup. Flings are fun, variety is fun, options are everywhere, and once you give in, it can be hard to stop. Forcing your mate into a phase of celibacy only further stacks the odds against you. A client once told me that though he'd originally begun hiring prostitutes because his wife wouldn't fuck him, he liked it so much that he wouldn't be willing to give it up even if she started. My takeaway from this was that if his fidelity meant more to her than her abstinence, his wife should have slept with him. But if it didn't, there wasn't really a problem.

Sam and I have gone through periods of sexual stress and disconnect, and those times upset me very much, in part because I worry it will lead to or is a sign of something rotten coming between us. But my sexual appreciation for him is lasting and profound. Without sex, I wouldn't have fallen in love with him. I was using Tinder in search of purely physical encounters, not dates. Without sex, we wouldn't have spent so much time together and probably wouldn't have met at all.

But I think it's true on a deeper level, too: I fell in love with who Sam was while he had sex with me, how he treated me, how he stayed intentional and funny and sweet at the height of his desire, how fervor didn't wipe out his consideration. Sex accelerates closeness because it creates conditions for intimacy to flourish, but that doesn't mean its moments of connection are as deceptive as they're sometimes made out to be—biological, chemical tricks to which women are especially susceptible. Mutual intimacy feels good, but it also feels different with different people, and I adored how it felt with Sam.

It seems crude to admit that I'm obsessed with his penis, but I've seen so many, and I like all sorts of them, but his is entirely perfect. Preference is subjective, of course, but his is so spectacular, it's like it was designed in a lab. And I love touching Sam. I think sometimes of the men I've been with who seem like they hadn't been touched in weeks or months, and in some spots, for years. I don't touch him out of duty; I do it because I like to and I want to, but part of why I want to is that I don't want him to be neglected like that. I want him to feel like each part of him is loved, as it is.

During our first trip to LA together, I dropped acid on the beach without telling him. He figured it out pretty quickly when my pupils went wide and I became transfixed by a child who ran in and out of the ocean, laughing as my fingers and toes kneaded the sand. I was afraid I loved him more than he loved me, a lot more, and that I always would. I'd been the better loved one before and I knew it could be tiresome and provoke meanness in the recipient. I was afraid he'd humiliate me and break my heart, and there didn't seem any good way to alleviate that fear, which was why I took the LSD. I just wanted a break from it.

At night, when we got back to the bungalow where we were staying, we went straight to bed. People sometimes claim that drug epiphanies don't last longer than the drug, but I haven't forgotten him naked on his knees in front of me and me sort of crouching below, my face at his thigh, struck with the certainty that I would not regret putting my mouth and hands on him and having him inside me because being naked with him was a blessing. I understood then that my enjoyment of his body was sacred and not meaningless, nor reliant on his deserving it or earning it in some way. They were gifts to me, the love and the attraction I felt, and his presence.

I wonder how I would respond if Sam cheated on me, and then I have to wonder what cheating on me would actually mean. Having sex with someone else? Having an emotional affair? I've worked at different times in our relationship, never at a volume approaching my previous days, but I've left for a night and come home to him hours later. I've gone away for days on trips. I know there are many contexts within which sex is meaningless and also that it can have meaning without becoming a hazard. One high-profile client was especially talkative over text, charming and flirty and attentive at a time when Sam and I were often apart because of our jobs. I felt so lonely and lost then that I would play single songs on repeat all day like I was trying to put myself in a trance or transport to another plane. I was depressed, but instead of medication, I used what I had on hand, and this client was good daydream material because of the lifestyle to which he was attached. But, weeks later, when we at last met for our date, I cried and cried over my folly. I was overwhelmed by how much better everything felt with Sam. The daydreams were worthless in comparison to what I had, what I have.

I don't want to deny Sam love or pleasure or any processes of self-discovery. If he had a fantastic one-night stand with someone and then never saw them again, I don't think it would automatically harm me. And if he had an emotional affair that he didn't consummate—or did, but I never noticed—isn't the not-noticing an indication that it isn't taking something from me, at least not taking something I couldn't spare? Or what if the change I noticed was his feeling good about himself and being sweeter to me? A year after we met, Roger wrote to me that a recent date of ours had put him in a very good mood and improved his attitude toward his wife when she complained to him about her work: "In the past, I have found some of the issues she frets over a bit trivial but this time I was in a position to be warm and supportive instead of cold, angry, and dismissive. Cold, angry, and dismissive would have been much more likely had I felt neglected and uncared-for."

I don't want Sam to fall in love with someone else because I worry that would make him fall out of love with me, but what if it didn't weaken our relationship—didn't make him love me less or fuck me less, didn't change his investment in our home and our family? The couples' therapist Esther Perel has a podcast episode in which a wife talks about wanting to stay with her husband despite his recently revealed affairs because those affairs hadn't kept him from being a good father or provider. He still had sex with her. She felt doted on and loved. None of that negated the pain, but it was enough to make her want to stay.

Back when Sam and I had met only a few times, I texted him something dirty that I wanted to do to him that night. I was on my way into town and anticipated meeting up, but he'd gotten the date confused or something, and since we hadn't done what I texted him about yet, he thought I sent him the message accidentally and that it was meant for someone else I was hooking up with. He didn't reply, which confused me and hurt my feelings, but I just changed the subject and only figured out what had gone wrong much later, when we were reminiscing about our first days.

"I thought about texting you, 'This is Sam,' to call you out," he said, "but I didn't."

"I wish you had," I said. We were laughing about it. "So I could have texted back, 'I know!'" I'd felt so rejected and vulnerable for no reason.

"I sat with it for a while, and asked myself why I was bothered," he said. "I told myself I was falling in love with you, and I knew there were others for you, but I thought, *That's okay, it's still good. It's still happy. This happens all the time. This is what people do.*"

I want to be with Sam, and I also don't want to limit him from living a full, satisfied life. What do I do if those desires conflict? My first instinct about the cheating question is that I just don't want to know. I don't want to forbid him from being romantic or sexual with other people and I also want to be totally ignorant if he does. I want it to be a secret from everyone, his coworkers and friends and neighbors, too.

I don't think Sam wants to be romantic or sexual with anyone else, and I think the suggestion—that he does or could or will— would hurt him. But how many wives of my clients thought the same about their husbands? How many husbands thought the same about themselves?

A FEW YEARS INTO our relationship, before we were married, Sam and I began having terrible fights. We'd had moments of rupture earlier on—misunderstandings, miscommunications, flare-ups of hurt that couldn't be explained by either of us doing anything bad, exactly. Those cracks made me worry I was wrong about what I'd felt, either wrong for feeling it or wrong for thinking—imagining—that I'd felt it, and then the worry became a crack, too. Those doubts required mutual tending, mutual tears, sex for reunion and proof, and frequently the end effect was for me to feel closer to him, stronger than when we started. In a drawing Sam made me, two egg shapes hug each other so hard that one knocks a chink out of the other, and from the small split, flowers grow.

But these later fights were serious clashes, conflicts that would keep me, if not both of us, up all night, and the sourness of unresolved disagreement lingered for weeks, months. The issue no longer seemed to be correctable misalignment and new-to-each-other ignorance but betrayal, selfishness, ill intent. *I'm sleeping somewhere else tonight* fights. *It shouldn't be this hard* fights. To him, I was insufficiently committed to riding out our ups and downs, while I believed he wasn't trying hard enough to keep us out of the downs altogether. We were both probably right. He valued constancy and I valued intensity, and neither of us were receiving as much as we needed.

Yet we stayed together, and the bitterness, for me anyway, has long since dissolved. Those struggles feel far away, a period of grave childhood illness that yielded to health and left only murky half-memories in its wake. We hurt each other during that period, but neither of us did anything unforgivable, and maybe what we did doesn't require forgiveness at all. It's as if a person drowning, in a panic, accidentally struck someone trying to save them, and we were both the other's victim and rescuer, and back on dry land, there is no animosity, just recovery and relief.

My inability to explain why we stayed together gnaws at me because the hostility and disappointment back then were so strong, I didn't think there was any cure for it. I can't stop asking myself what I would now tell someone in a similar position to the position I was in then, someone who asks, "How did you know? Why didn't you break up? Should I stick it out?" I don't know how I knew; I don't even know that I knew. I'd like to think I did, but maybe I didn't. Did we stay together because we were meant for each other and we each intuited or decided that? Or did we stick it out because one or both of us was too attached to let the other go, though the signs said we should? Luck seems to have played a terrifyingly prominent role in our union and in my life as a whole. Maybe we just got lucky.

For a time, I approached romantic union as a board on which every light could be lit but isn't thrown by a single switch. Sometimes sex comes first, and it somehow prevents the emotional intimacy bulb from blinking on, or friendship precedes and precludes sex. Or the friendship bulb warms up for years before the sex circuit can connect, or the sex bulb blazes bright, burns out, and is never replaced, though commitment and love stay lit. When I was a girl basking in platonic intimacy with boys, I thought there might be one foolproof pattern, a particular approach or act or attitude that would illuminate everything at once: respect, candor, commitment, lust. After so much questing for experience, I don't think there is. Complete affinity is rare, and the socially mandated trouble between men and women pushes it even further into the horizon. But rare isn't impossible.

As I got older I was exposed to critiques of the insistence that a single person can or should satisfy another's every need, and through work I participated in the marital triangulation of appetite and urge. I see the wisdom there. But I also saw how many men fuse their vulnerability and tenderness to sex so that neither you nor they can access one without the other. I saw, too, how many tried to cordon off sex from any well of fellow-feeling and capacity for connection.

I monitor which switches Sam and I have thrown at any time because of what I witnessed at work and learned from my parents' divorce, and also because I am a woman and appointed custodian of relational health. What could we lose and still be us? Physical intimacy? What could we introduce and still be us? Major secrets? I want to be close to my husband. That's why I married him. But I don't want to control him or to lock us into behaviors that served us once but don't anymore. What could change before there's more distance between us than desire? Can that ever be discovered in advance, or is it only learned the hard way?

There are answers I don't have, but there are also truths that have stood like mountains since the beginning. That Sam is generous and gentle and kind. That looking at his face makes me feel shy because I like it so much. That I want his body against mine while I sleep and often when I'm awake, and that I love the objects he makes me, the notes he writes me, the art he gives me, the surprises of his mind. That I like his smell.

The fact I come back to amid uncertainty is this: I love nothing more than I love Sam's laugh. When he laughs, it has my full attention. I hear it and look to find his face, and once I do, I stare and listen the way a baby watches something others forget to be dazzled by. I do this high, I do this sober, I do this when we are with friends and when we are alone, because his smile gives me mine.

There it is, my favorite thing. The joy of my life. His happiness.

ACKNOWLEDGMENTS

I first thank my agent, Samantha Shea, and my editor, Carina Guiterman, without whom this book would not exist.

Thank you, Melissa Gira Grant, Jo Livingstone, and Lola Pellegrino, for your intelligence, humor, thoughtfulness, and friendship.

Jamie Hood and Harron Walker, I love you so much. I can't imagine a world in which I wrote this without you, and I don't want to. Thank you for being in my life.

And to Sam: I'll thank you in person.

CHARLOTTE SHANE is the author of the memoir *Prostitute Laundry* and a cofounder of TigerBee Press.